Seeds

SEEDS OF CONSCIOUSNESS

The Wisdom of
Sri Nisargadatta Maharaj

EDITED BY JEAN DUNN

The Acorn Press
Durham, North Carolina

Translated from the Marathi by Ramesh S. Balsekar,
Damayanti Dungaji, S. V. Sapre, Saumitra K. Mullarpattan,
and by Mr. Patan.

First published by Grove Press, Inc., New York, 1982.
Pubished by The Acorn Press, 1990; reprinted 1997, 2004,
2007, 2015.

ISBN: 0-89386-025-5
Library of Congress Catalog Card Number: 89-81146.

Cover photograph © by Jitendra Arya.

Printed in the United States of America.

A Date with Eternity

Praise be to Nisargadatta Maharaj, great mystic of Bharat!

Outwardly he looked like a common householder and spoke only his native language, Marathi, but the wisdom of his spontaneous utterances was the same as the wisdom found in the Vedas and the Upanishads. He was a shining example of one who is in the consummate state of Eternal Awareness. To a sincere seeker—one wanting to meet a living sage equalling in wisdom those in the scriptures—he represented the fulfillment of his innermost yearnings.

Sri Nisargadatta Maharaj did not pose as a Mahatma, a Bhagavan, or a Paramahamsa. He had no yoga, no system of philosophy to offer or preach; all he knew and experienced was Real Nature—the Real Nature common to himself and his listeners. He gave the same clarion call which from time immemorial India has given to the whole of humanity: "Know your Real Self!"

For forty years and more this great man kept repeating, "Be aware of your state of being—pure and simple being—without being this or that or the other." He challenged his listener to ask questions, but his answers were never merely answers. Each time the answer would be a challenge to the questioner to find out for himself what his Real Nature was.

He spoke from his own direct insight and would say that he only tells his own "story." He needed no proof for his statements. He was not anxious to cite any authority for them so that the listener might better appreciate their truth. He also urged his questioner to speak only from his own experience and not to quote from what others have said. He maintained that his own "story" would also become that of his listener, that just as it had unfolded in him, it was bound to unfold for his listener—once he stabilized in his own "beingness," his *pure* state of consciousness.

When the vexing question of former lives was brought up Maharaj would immediately ask if the questioner knew anything about this, his *present*, "birth." "Why ask a question that is completely unnecessary?" he would say. "Why indeed? When the Buddha was asked what sin is, the Buddha replied, 'All that is unnecessary is sin.' The only thing necessary is to find out *who* is asking the question. What is your Real Nature? What is the Reality that is there before this 'I-am' consciousness arose? Stay put in your beingness, and then you will see what is prior to the words 'I am.' "

From a study of the Vedas, the Upanishads, and innumerable other Hindu scriptures a student can get a glimpse of Truth—as if viewing a beautiful, true-to-life painting of Truth. But sitting close to Nisargadatta Maharaj and listening to the living Upanishad was to be in the presence of bright and vibrant Truth itself.

Dr. Damayantie Doongagi
Bombay

Introduction

When I was asked to "introduce" Sri Nisargadatta Maharaj to the readers of this book, I was rather taken aback because I would hardly have considered myself eligible. Before I could marshal in my mind the arguments why someone else should perform this very honorable task, I was told that Maharaj would like me to do it. Then, of course, the matter ended without more arguments.

I had always felt, deep in my bones, that there had to be something deeper to religion than praying to one of the Gods to give us happiness and to keep misery away. I had read a reasonable amount on Advaita philosophy; so when I first came across the book *I Am That* [1] containing dialogues collected by the late Sri Maurice Frydman between Sri Nisargadatta Maharaj and various people who had visited him, I was considerably surprised that a Master should have lived, not in the Himalayas, but in my hometown of Bombay, and that, in spite of my deep interest in the subject, I should not have had the good fortune, all these years, to meet him. Immediately after that, needless to say, I went and sat at his feet. (Actually, it was through an article by Ms. Jean Dunn in the October, 1978, issue of *The Mountain Path* that I first came to know of Maharaj, but it was reading the book that chiefly influenced me.)

That first visit, when I climbed up the steps to the loft of his ground-floor residence in Vanamali Mansion, at 10th Lane, Khetwadi, I found Maharaj seated in one corner of the room, lighting some agarbatties [joss sticks] and placing them in the several receptacles in front of him. When I bowed down before him in salutation, and placed before

[1] Chetana Pvt. Ltd., Bombay; 3d. ed. 1981. Published in the U.S.A. by The Acorn Press, Durham, NC.

him the offering of fruits, he looked at me with his piercing gaze, then smiled at me warmly and said: "Ah, you have come, have you? Do sit down." For a moment I could not help wondering if he had mistaken me for someone else, because his words seemed to imply that he was expecting me. When he asked me if I had any specific queries I said I would very much like to sit quietly and absorb both his words and the spiritual atmosphere that prevailed in his presence. He smiled and nodded. Since then I have visited Maharaj regularly.

It has been my experience that Maharaj is reluctant to talk about himself as an individual, and any personal information about him had to be collected from others. One thing is certain: he is not a Sadhu or Sanyasi; actually he does not have any particular pose at all. He is a simple man, dresses in the most ordinary clothes, and looks the simple family man that he is, exactly like millions of others. Indeed, during his talks, he often says that he is not a learned person, that therefore he can talk only from his personal knowledge or experience, and that whatever he has been able to know about his true being applies to everyone else. I shall never forget a particular sentence of his: "At one time I considered myself a male human being, got married and had children; then I met my Guru, and under his initiation and instruction, came to know that I am Brahman."

Sri Nisargadatta Maharaj was "born" in Bombay as Maruti Shivrampant Kampli, in March, 1897. His birthday coincided with the auspicious day of Hanuman Jayanti; hence the name Maruti. Young Maruti's childhood was spent at Kandalgaon, a village some distance from Bombay, to which his father had moved in "the year of the plague." I remember Maharaj saying that perhaps his earliest personal recollection is being carried on his father's shoulders, heading toward a hill just as the sun was peeping over the top. In the course of time, income from the farm was insufficient to maintain the family. After their father's death in 1915, first the eldest son, and then Maruti himself, had to go back to Bombay to earn the family livelihood. Maruti started his

career as a clerk with a private firm, but with his independent and adventurous temperament, he soon took to trading
on his own. (It is one of those many coincidences that I have
noticed since my association with Maharaj, that immediately after I had written this particular paragraph—in fact,
the very next day—Maharaj happened to mention that he
was always so independent by nature that he could never
bear pressure of any kind from any one: "Better one day of
independence than a lifetime without freedom." He gave
me a knowing smile. This was one of those rare occasions
when Maharaj spoke about his personal life.)

Maruti Kampli started his business venture with one
shop making and selling bidis [hand-made local cigarettes],
and in a comparatively short period became the owner of
eight such shops. In 1924 he married. There were four children—one son and three daughters. His mere material pros-
perity could not bring Maruti much contentment. A deeply
religious atmosphere and ritualistic tradition in the family
generally, and his early association at Kandalgaon with a
learned Brahimin named Vishnu Gore in particular, had kin-
dled in him, quite early in life, the inevitable questions regarding the relationship between Man, the World outside,
and God. It was to a friend of his, one Yeshwantrao Bagkar,
that Maruti owed his introduction to Sri Siddharameshwar
Maharaj of the Navanath Sampradaya. Bagkar was well
aware of Maruti's sincere and intense quest for Truth, and
one day decided to take him to his Guru. As Maharaj put it:
"Bagkar practically forced me to accompany him when he
went to Siddharameshwar Maharaj. Even the traditional gar-
land of flowers which the disciple places round the Guru's
neck was purchased by Bagkar, who, according to the dic-
tates of destiny, practically pushed me down on the Guru's
feet." Soon thereafter, Maruti received his initiation from
his Guru and pursued his spiritual activities with his native
zeal and determination until they culminated in his attaining realization. This happened between 1933 and 1936.

Sri Siddharameshwar Maharaj took Mahasamadhi in
1936. The following year, Sri Nisargadatta Maharaj suddenly

decided to abandon his family and his prosperous business and wander about the country. After visiting several holy places and temples in Southern India, when he was on his way to the North to spend the rest of his life in the Himalayas, he happened to meet a fellow disciple. After a discussion with him, Sri Nisargadatta Maharaj came to the conclusion that such wanderings were really not necessary and that an active life of dispassionate action was far more meaningful. Perhaps it was the good fortune of the thousands of people who were since able to get Maharaj's guidance that brought him back to Bombay. When he returned to Bombay, he found all his shops but one had been lost, but calmly decided that it sufficed for his worldly needs. Since then everything has been happening spontaneously, nothing is being done with deliberate intention or conscious effort.

As he would sit at his bidi shop transacting his business quietly and efficiently, some friend would come to see him and the talk would always be on the same subject, Paramartha—the ultimate meaning. Such talks received so much publicity by word of mouth that there would always be a small crowd outside the little shop listening to the pearls of wisdom. So when his son was able to take charge of the shop, Maharaj retired to the loft he had constructed in his residence for his personal use, and which has since quietly assumed the holiness of an Ashram.

Before I go on to my personal experience with Maharaj, I will mention one significant incident in his life. Occasionally Maharaj makes a reference to the moment of death and to how such an experience which is traumatic to an ordinary person becomes one of great ecstasy to a Dhnyani. Sometimes he says he knows this because he has witnessed his own death! I made some inquiries and this is the incident to which apparently he refers:

Every Sunday evening, some years ago, there used to be a Bhajan program at the resident of Sri Bhainath Maharaj [Sri Sabnis], one of Maharaj's fellow disciples, and Maharaj would invariably attend. One Sunday a disciple of Maharaj

called at his home to take him to Sri Sabnis's residence, and
found Maharaj obviously ill in bed and the family members
very anxious. Maharaj did not want to have a doctor examine him: He suggested that the disciple go to Sri Sabnis and
ask him to carry on with the usual program. But the disciple
would not move from Maharaj's side, and ultimately Sri Sabnis arrived to find out what had happened. Maharaj insisted
that Sri Sabnis and the disciple go back and complete the
usual Bhajan program. They reluctantly complied, but returned as soon as the program was over, along with several
other disciples. They were delighted to find Maharaj sitting
up and very much improved. A few days later, in one of his
talks, Maharaj narrated that that afternoon he was actually
witnessing his own death, and that it was a most ecstatic
moment.

The daily routine of Maharaj for several years now has
been simple and regular: dialogues with visitors morning and
afternoon, for about 90 minutes each time, and Bhajans four
times a day, in accordance with his Guru's instructions. During the talks/dialogues, the gathering these days normally
consists of about twenty persons, increasing to perhaps
thirty-five on Sundays and holidays to fill the small area to
capacity. Quite a few are usually foreigners who have come
from long distances, not as tourists but specifically "to get
his darshan" and listen to his talks, because after reading *I
Am That* they could not resist the desire to meet him. Some
of the visitors, both Indians and foreigners, have been persons of outstanding intelligence and successful leaders in
their respective fields. "Is it not a miracle of my Guru's
Grace," says Maharaj, "that eminent people, who would
normally be unapproachable by a small man like me, come
here with folded hands to hear the talks? Is it me as an
individual that they come to see, or is it the outpouring of
my Guru's Grace that they come to hear?"

Maharaj's residence occasionally attracts persons who
wish to exhibit their own book learning and who try to draw
Maharaj into unfruitful discussions. While Maharaj does
not hesitate to give short shrift to such people when they

transgress a certain limit, to the others who have come with a sincere desire to understand him and approach him with simple humility, he shows an astonishing amount of patience and tolerance. Whatever Maharaj says comes out with such quick spontaneity, calm assertion, and cool authority that one cannot but instinctively feel the presence of the Master, and recognize TRUTH even if one may not quite understand it then! He never quotes any authorities to justify or to support his statements, not even the Vedas. He obviously speaks from a level beyond words, which the Vedas are incapable of talking about.

Maharaj often makes it clear that those who go to him in the hope of advice that could bring material benefit or relief from physical disability or mental solace will be disappointed, because he never discusses such matters. Perhaps it is because of this that Maharaj has not become a "popular" Guru. Those who expect a confirmation of their own favorite concepts or forms of religion would not only be disappointed but may even feel aggrieved and frustrated by some of Maharaj's statements, for instance: "All scriptures say that before the world was, the Creator was. But who knows the Creator? He alone who was before the Creator—your own real being, the Source of all the Worlds and their Creators." Actually Maharaj's teaching has no direct basis in any established religion. "Can any one tell me," he asks, "the religion of each of the five elements?"

What then does Maharaj teach? As Maharaj himself often says, all that he does is to present to us a spiritual mirror in which we could, if we seriously wished to, see our true image. If one could venture to do so, his basic teaching could perhaps be summed up as follows:

The entire universe [Mahadakash] exists only in Consciousness [Chidakash], while the Dhnyani has his stand in the Absolute [Paramakash]. In the Absolute—pure beingness—there is no Consciousness of "I Am"; it is prior to thoughts and words. Then, for no apparent reason, Consciousness spontaneously stirs into existence. In Consciousness the world appears and disappears. All there is, is Me; all there is, is Mine; before all beginnings, after all endings, I AM. Whatever happens, I must be there to witness it. Therefore, it is not that the world does not exist. The world is an appearance in consciousness which is the totality of the known in the immensity of the unknown. What begins and ends is mere appearance. The World can be said to APPEAR but not BE.

Maharaj tells us that whenever every single individual dreams, he has the actual experience of the world being created in consciousness. When a person is not fully awake, and consciousness merely stirs, he dreams; and in his dream, in that tiny spot of consciousness, in a split second, is created an entire world exactly similar to the world outside, and in that world are seen the earth, the sun, hills and rivers, and people (including himself!) behaving exactly as in the world outside. While the person is dreaming the dream world is very much real: his experiences—both pleasure and pain—are extremely realistic. But once he wakes up, the entire dream world merges in the consciousness in which it was created. In the waking state, says Maharaj, the world emerges because of ignorance [Maya] and takes you into a waking dream state. Both sleep and waking are misnomers because you are only dreaming; you dream that you are awake, you dream that you are asleep. Only the Dhnyani knows true waking and true sleeping. See all as a dream, and stay out of it. . . . The main point to grasp is that you have projected onto yourself a world of your own imagination, based on memories, desires, and fears, and that you have imprisoned yourself in it. Realize that, break the spell, and BE FREE.

The Creation of the World, the appearance in Consciousness, has several aspects: the parent principle is the Prakriti-Purusa, the male and female duality; the material of creation is the essence [Satva] of the five elements; the Satva acts through the two other Gunas [attributes]—Rajas [energy] and Tamas [inertia and ego]. An individual may think that it is he who acts, but truly all activity is accomplished by the five elements through the three Gunas. It is Satva that wakes one up into Consciousness; Rajas that pushes one into the daily activity; Tamas that makes one assume the doership of the activity.

For the serious student, Maharaj's approach is direct, forceful, and simple, though at the same time deep and subtle:

(A) Suppose some water accumulates; after a time, the body of an insect forms itself; it begins to move; it KNOWS that it exists. A piece of bread is thrown in a corner and is left there for a time; soon the form of a worm makes its appearance; it begins to move; it KNOWS that it exists. The egg of a hen, after the application of the body heat for a certain time, suddenly breaks open and a little chick appears; it begins to move; it KNOWS that it exists. The sperm of the man germinates in the womb of the woman, and after the nine-month period is delivered as the baby, and begins to go through the states of sleeping and waking, and carries out the physical functions; after a few months, the same sperm, now in the form of an infant, begins to KNOW that it exists, and starts acquiring further information from the mother, that it is a boy or girl, etc., etc.

(B) In these four cases—the insect, the worm, the chicken, and the human body—what is really born? Is it not, says Maharaj, the knowledge "I AM," the Consciousness that is really born, along with the two states of sleeping and waking? This Consciousness—identical in all four cases—which has suddenly appeared in each of the four types of forms, finding itself without any kind of "support," takes resort in the particular physical form and identifies with it. In other words, what was originally without any shape or form, the message "I AM"—the mere knowledge of existence *generally* (not anyone in particular)—has mistakenly identified itself with one particular body, accepted its birth, and thereafter lives in the constant shadow of the terror of "death."

(C) This "I AM-ness," this consciousness without which, as Maharaj says, one would not know that one exists—and which, therefore, everyone loves most and would preserve at any cost as long as possible—is the only "capital" one is born with. This Consciousness cannot exist without a physical form, which is merely the consequence of the germination of the father's sperm, which is itself the essence of the food consumed by the parents. This is the analysis of the process which has resulted in the birth of an individual body containing Consciousness, a process for the start of which the concerned "individual" has never been consulted! If one thus clearly sees the process of what has come into existence, can there be any room for an individual personality in which one could take pride, something which is merely a bundle of memories and habits, without any substance?

(D) If, then, there can really be no individual personality, the question arises: for whom is there any liberation or Moksha? It is only in the case of the human being that this question arises, because no other form of life has the intelligence to question its own existence or source.

Liberation comes about, says Maharaj, when the knowledge "I AM" realizes:

(I) That it has *always* been unlimited and totally free, and that it is itself the cause of all creation—if there is no consciousness, there can be no world.

(II) That it has, however, created its own shackles of bondage by self-limitation—by identifying itself with the individual body.

(III) That it has no form or design—that it is the "quality" of the food essence (which has taken the shape of the body), like the quality of sweetness in sugar.

(IV) That, when the food essence (the body) becomes old and "dies," its quality, the knowledge "I AM," also disappears—i.e., being no longer subject to the three Gunas, becomes NIRGUNA, and merges with REALITY. Who dies?!

Maharaj repeatedly sums up his teaching by asking his listeners to go beyond his words "BACK TO THE SOURCE" and abide there—the Source being REALITY, one's true state, prior to the arrival of Consciousness, when there were no needs of any kind, the state prior to the illusion of the stream of events (like an illness in a normally healthy body)—conception, birth of the body, a lifetime, and finally the death of the body. "You" are always separate from the entire "happening," merely witnessing it; the witnessing ceases at the end of the happening: who dies?!

To know with definite conviction, says Maharaj, that you are neither in the body nor in the mind, though aware of both, is already self-knowledge. Liberation is not a matter of acquisition, but a matter of faith and conviction that you have ALWAYS been FREE, and a matter of courage to act on this conviction. There is nothing to change; it is only when the very idea of changing is seen as false that the changeless can come into its own!

Maharaj's listeners are struck by the wholly different approach in his teachings. For instance, on the subject of love, the usual teaching has always been that there cannot be any spiritual progress unless one develops a feeling of love for others. This approach could quite easily be a matter of frustration to an honest seeker who knows that he does not—and cannot—love others like himself. What a relief, therefore, when Maharaj says: "Be true to your own self. Love yourself absolutely. Do not pretend that you love others as yourself. Unless you have realized others as one with yourself, you cannot love them. Don't pretend to be what you are not, don't refuse to be what you are. Your love for others is the result of self-knowledge, not its cause."

And finally, what an encouragement to hear Maharaj say: "What you have learned here becomes the seed. You may forget it apparently. But it will live, and in due season sprout and grow and bring forth flowers and fruits. All will happen by itself. You need not do anything: only, don't prevent it."

Ramesh S. Balsekar
March 31, 1980

TALKS
WITH
MAHARAJ

July 7, 1979

Maharaj: In Nisarga [nature] everything is time-bound (seasons, sowing, reaping, etc.), but nature itself is not time-bound. Nature is neither male nor female. Many Avatars come and go, but nature is not affected. The story of nature is emanating from all the impressions taken in your mind since birth. So long as you are holding on to these memories there will be no knowledge of Self. If you just study whatever has happened in nature, like history, great lives, etc., you cannot realize your Self. You have to go within. Whatever great things have happened in nature, however powerful, still they disappear right here. These situations appear and disappear. This is actually abstract, what is solid here is the knowledge "I AM." The seen and the seeing disappear. I tell this only to those who are prepared to listen. Whatever appears is bound to disappear. The greatest appearance is the knowledge "I AM." It is invisible before the birth and after the death of the body, and while it is visible it is a solid thing. Many great Sages have appeared and disappeared because of the powerful seed "I AM." When the prana leaves the body, knowledge has no support and it disappears, i.e., it is unseen.

What I am expounding is very deep. You may experience Brahma even, but that experience will not remain. All experiences are due to the cell "I AM." Both the cell and the experience will disappear. Even the best of your memories will vanish one day. The knowledge "I AM" is time-bound, all your knowledge sprouts from the concept that you are.

Millions of Sages have come and gone. Do they presently experience the state of "I AM"? They had no authority to perpetuate their beingness; their "I Amness" became unseen. The Sages cannot make an iota of change in the world. Whatever happens, happens.

Questioner: But Maharaj has said that because of the existence of a Jnani the world is benefited.

M: It is said to an ignorant one, one who clings to the body-mind. When there is no "I Amness" what is it that you need?

Q: I am lost.

M: Who is talking? To whom?

Q: To myself.

M: If you (the knowledge "I am") are really lost, how will you know about the sense of being lost? You are carried away by concepts. This infinitesimal seed contains the universe. You miss the point, you do not understand me properly. This principle "I Am" I am telling you about again and again.

Find out your identity. Whatever appears is going to disappear. What can Roosevelt or Gandhi do now? In the very places which they were commanding changes have taken place. Why don't they talk? When the prana leaves the body even great Sages cannot speak.

Q: In the Gita, Sri Krishna says that wherever there is calamity and there is no dharma, he will come and restore.

M: This is like the seasons, the cycle is there. In this cycle the deeper meaning of the Self is to be understood. All questions will be over once you solve the riddle of "I Am."

Q: Sometimes I feel good and sometimes bad, sometimes blissful, sometimes depressed. I know this is the mind; the Vedas say that mind is born out of the moon and hence it changes.

M: Oblige me, after coming here, by leaving your mind aside. Good and bad are in the realm of the mind only. Disown whatever you get from the mind.

Q: Who tells me to come here and be at your feet?

M: It cannot be said in words; you can call it anything you like. Moon means mind, mind is like a liquid stuff as it flows continuously. Just innocently, dispassionately, observe the mind flow; do not own the mind flow. Be in the "I Amness" state without words. You give meaning to words

and in the end words go; finally the perceptibles and observ-
ables go into the non-perceptible and non-observable state.
Find that out. You will understand this slowly and get peace
and rest. You do not do anything. It happens. You talk
about knowledge, that knowledge is what you have read and
heard from others. Unless you have confidence in your own
Self you have to draw upon the authority of others, but I tell
you from my real state; as I experience it, as I see it, I speak,
without citing the authority of the Gita or Mahabharata.
When you talk about the Gita you must know that it relates
to you, every word of it relates to your own Self.

July 22, 1979

Questioner: Are consciousness and the witness the same?
Maharaj: For whatever is visible the consciousness is the
witness. There is another principle which witnesses consciousness, and this principle is beyond the world.

Q: How do you witness consciousness?

M: How do you witness the fact that you are sitting?
Effortlessly or with effort?

Q: Effortlessly.

M: The same way. Whenever you put in effort is from
the bodily standpoint. The knowledge "I Am" is the soul of
the entire world. The witness of the knowledge "I Am" is
prior to the knowledge "I Am." Try to understand yourself
as you are, do not add any qualifications. Just as you prepare
various dishes out of various ingredients, you want to make
something. Witnessing or awareness is just as you observe
your deep sleep. Just like that.

Q: I do not understand.

M: It is not understandable. You must contemplate
yourself. Whatever comes on the screen of contemplation
will surely disappear. The Contemplator remains.

Q: Is not the Contemplator also a concept of mind?

M: Concept and mind are beams of light from the Contemplator.

Q: Is "I Am" the sum total of everything you perceive?

M: Yes. "I Amness" spontaneously appears and disappears; it has no dwelling place. It is like a dream world. Do not try to be something, even a spiritual person. You are the manifested. The tree is already there in the seed. Such is this "I Am." Just see it as it is. Do not try to interfere with what you see. Having understood this, what could be your need?

Q: Nothing.

M: You must stabilize in this conviction. Knowledge [jnana] is the soul of the whole universe. Do not get involved with siddhis [spiritual powers]. Although you may not purposely go in for siddhis, around you some miracles may happen. Do not claim the authorship of them. A devotee of yours who is at a distance of a thousand kilometers from you can have your darshan in form. Whenever your devotee praises your knowledge, the knowledge takes concrete shape. Do not think that you are doing something. Sound fills the entire space; similarly, the knowledge "I Am" will fill the entire place. Once you understand this there is no death for you. If you think yourself an individual you will surely have death.

A spiritual seeker wants to be something; just be as you are. If people come to you, then automatically words come out of you. Although you may not have studied the Vedas, whatever comes out of you will be the same as what is in the Vedas and Upanishads. At the time of speaking you will not have the slightest idea that you are a Jnani or a knowledgeable person.

Q: I am feeling the burden of "I Amness." How to get rid of it?

M: Where is the question of getting rid of it when you have not planted it?

Q: I know, but my mind feels that I should get rid of it.

M: Can the mind recognize the highest principle? Do not follow the mind; mind is following its own natural course. You get identified with the mind and speak for it.

With what insistence can the mind make changes in the sky or space?

The space is the eyeglass of the "I Am" through which it observes the world. The five senses cannot know you, you know the five senses.

Q: By "you" what do you mean? Which "you"?

M: Since you feel duality, I mean the listener in you.

Q: I am not outside consciousness.

M: Actually you are out of it, and recognize it. If you say that you are consciousness, then you are the entire world. You are separate from "I Am." "I Am" is itself an illusion. The knowledge "I Am" and the world are tricks of Maya. There is no substance to them. There are no words actually, you speak words for your satisfaction.

You know that there are hunger, thirst, waking and sleep states. Without these, what are you? You think that these are all your eternal needs; this is the trick of Mula Maya [primary illusion]. "I Amness" has a certain span of time. How long will you be associated with these?

Q: Memory makes the world seem real. Unless memory registers the color green, there is no color green.

M: Memory is inside "I Am." Relative repetition is the play of Maya. If you are not able to sleep for eight days will you survive?

Q: No.

M: That is, you will be beyond the waking and sleep states; in short, the illusion will vanish.

Q: When I get up in the mornings where does the "I Am" consciousness come from?

M: You are not able to understand it. Like a film, it is already there and is reproducing. This chemical is called the greatest principle by the Vedas; it is the Hiranyagarbha [golden womb]. "I Amness" is forgotten in deep sleep and it appears in the waking and dream states.

Q: How do I remember the previous things?

M: It is the skill of the "I Amness." What identity do you hold for yourself?

Q: I am the witness.

M: Of what?

Q: All the activities of the body-mind.

M: This is the quality of the body-mind only and is not the Self knowledge. Worms appear in stale food. Similarly, the body is stale food; the Self wriggles in it. When the body is decomposing, the worm "I Amness" is at work. The taste is "I Amness," which it enjoys without a tongue. We take too much pride in the taste of this stale food. What knowledge do you want?

Q: My true Self.

M: As long as you think that the body is you, you will not get true knowledge. In Marathi there is a phrase, "borrowed wife," she who has to be returned. Similarly, this body is a borrowed thing; you have to return it. This identity with the body has to go.

Q: How is one to be successful in getting rid of this identification?

M: Try to investigate deep sleep and waking states. These are time-bound. Without the experience of waking and sleep states, try to explain what you are.

Q: Then I am wordless.

M: Are you sure? The Vedas also said "This is not," That is not," and at the end kept quiet, as it is beyond words. Without deep sleep and waking states do you know that you are, or do you experience "I Am"?

Q: No.

M: What is born: yourself or the two states? You will be liquidated soon if you come here. What will you pick out of these states as yourself?

Q: Nothing.

August 12, 1979

Maharaj: Are you satisfied?

Questioner: Sometimes there is satisfaction, sometimes not.

M: Who says this? Who tells you this?

Q: I see satisfaction, a feeling in consciousness. I am indifferent. Whatever is happening, whatever appears in my consciousness, I'm not concerned, I'm not interested. I have nothing to do with it.

M: It is not called indifference, it is detachment. There is no such thing as unhappiness. You don't worry about anything; that is the state, the real state. You feel no attraction toward anything in this world?

Q: Whatever is happening, there is no gaining, no losing.

M: How did this happen?

Q: I don't know.

M: Don't behave as others do, just because they say so. After hearing these teachings you should behave like a king or a lord. That should be your behavior, inwardly and outwardly. Aham Brahmasmi, "I am the Lord." Have you understood or not?

Q: I don't know.

M: Do you want to ask anything more?

Q: There is a great pressure in this feeling of being aware of myself. It is always accompanied by a great pressure in the head.

M: You should be a witness of that. You are aware of the consciousness, so you are beyond that. You are a witness of that.

Q: That feeling is there all the time.

M: Your consciousness is not in the body. There is attraction to that body yet, so that feeling has not gone completely. Your consciousness has some attraction, some love for your body; therefore that pressure is there.

You know your consciousness, you witness your consciousness now. Formerly that was not true because you were considering yourself as a body. Now you know that you are not the body. You know also that you are not the consciousness.

Formerly, before you heard this, before you came to India, your name for consciousness was the mind. Now the word for consciousness is Jnana [knowledge].

M [to another]: So your purpose is served, you are satisfied?

Q: Oh yes, a long time ago, when I left here.

M: After having had many experiences, you have now come to the conclusion that what preceded the experiences is the same. You are not affected by the experiences that take place in the world?

Q: Yes, I have come to that conclusion.

M: All the attractions of the world are just ordinary things to you? You are not affected by them? Have you attained that state? Or are you still craving for the respect of others, are you still craving for more knowledge of more arts?

Q: I can no longer hold that, so I am not craving it. I have nothing with which to retain it, but, who knows, if I found something with which to hold it, I might.

M: Craving means that you think that it has some benefits, some opportunities.

Q: It is fruitless, it all cancels out in the end; so it is useless.

M: So, you have seen everything, understood everything. What is it that prevails in the end?

Q: What prevails is not perceivable.

M: What is there which is primary? What is at the root?

Q: What is at the root is not an object.

M: You have realized that?

Q: No, I did not realize it, because it is greater than I. How could I see it?

M: When you are going through various experiences, do you realize that there is something which was prevailing right from the beginning of which you were not aware? Do you become aware of something which is much greater than all these experiences? If you have found that, can you stay with it? Or are you still passing through the experiences?

Q: I am not passing through the experiences, and, yes, I can stay with it. It's like when you are on a boat: you don't think that the water is moving—you know that the boat is moving—but you are aware that the water is there. You don't have to repeat to yourself, "Oh yes, I am moving on the water." What is there moves; underneath is what you move on.

M: When you are passing through all this, do you realize that it is all artificial, that it is not the real? What do you experience?

Q: I experience that I am passing through my own self-created projection.

M: Don't you see that what you realize as the illusion, the projection, is nothing but your own very small modification of your own Self?

Q: Oh yes.

M: When you realize this, don't you get a glimpse of what is the most ancient? The unlimited?

Q: I am not limited by the experience, or by the limitations of the experience.

M: The world is ever-changing, ever new, but it is nothing but the thoughts of the ancient, the trick of the ancient. So where is the question of your not being limited? Are you denying its existence?

Q: No, I am not denying its existence, I'm denying its reality.

M: Suppose you have a child and that child goes to Timbuktu and becomes its king. He will still be your child, don't you see?

Whatever is happening, the witness of that happening must be there to say that it is happening. The ancestor of all action must be there to watch that action so that he can narrate it.

Q: That witness, is it the Absolute or is it in consciousness? There must be someone who witnesses that experience?

M: I am not telling about this witness. I'm telling you about the core, that core ancestor of ours.

Out of a berry, out of the very forest of shrubs with berries, all these shrubs have grown. Because of that single berry.

What is that principle which observes the creation and the state prior to the creation? The Absolute. The no-being-ness state, the no-consciousness state alone knows that there is a consciousness. That no-"I Amness" state.

Many people will tell you about your mind inclinations, the mind flow, the activities in the realm of consciousness. That if you do this, you will get this; but has anyone told you of the state prior to the consciousness?

The lowest state (on the spiritual path) is that of the mumukshu. The mumukshu is one who has made a beginning in the spiritual search and he identifies with the body-mind. He always tried to derive benefits or gains or losses out of the body-mind sense. He meets a Guru and the Guru tells him, "You are not the body-mind, you are the manifest 'I Amness.'" "I Am" is the manifest world and that he realizes. He establishes himself there and finds that he is not the body-mind, he is the manifestation; in due course, he also realizes, "I am not that 'I Amness,' I am not that consciousness nor the manifest world, but I am the Absolute." Why are you quiet? Is it because of confusion or because you have no confusion and have attained that quietude?

Q: Is this state of "I Amness manifest" detachment?

M: What do you call that "I Amness"?

Q: Consciousness.

M: Do you know the consciousness? Do you witness the consciousness?

Q: I don't know.

M: To what principle do you give that name?

Q: Everything that I perceive or know. Everything.

M: Who knows consciousness?

Q: I don't know.

M: What you don't know, that is the prior-most.

Q: It seems, in consciousness the experiences constantly change, and, at the same time, something remains the same.

M: In ignorance you used to call it mind, but that is itself the knowledge of manifestation, that is the power of manifestation, this knowledge. It is the source of manifestation [Mula-maya]. It is Mahesvara, that is the highest Iswara principle whose name is Atman.

Q: Whose name?

M: The feeling you have of "I Amness"—"I Am" without words—that is Atman. It is very dynamic and moving. The consciousness is the mind of the Absolute; the power of knowledge, the power of memory, the message of "I Amness."

Q: The state of manifestation—is that a state of attachment?

M: Its happening or creating is spontaneous, without attachment, but once it appeared the attachment started.

You are all keeping quiet and not daring to ask questions.

Q: Questions are prepared before; when you come here they fade away.

M: In the womb of ignorance the knowledge was there and that knowledge, in maturity, had become this manifestation, but prior to ignorance that great ancestor is there.

You have the knowledge of knowing only on the basis of no-knowing. First of all, you do not know; on that no-knowing platform this knowing sprouts, but the basis is ignorance only. Although ignorance, when it grows into maturity, becomes knowledge, and becomes profuse in its manifestation, still its ancestor is ignorance only. Prior to ignorance is that ancestral state of Absolute.

Q: What are the signs to recognize a Jnani?

M: To think that one is a Jnani, knowledgeable, or full of wisdom, is folly. Once one presumes that he is full of wisdom he wants social recognition, he wants a status: that is the folly.

Who is a Jnani? The Jnani himself does not know he is and who is to recognize whom? Out of no-action, spontaneously, millions of creations are happening every moment and there is so much of chaos. Will a Jnani allow such a thing to happen?

The Jnani understands that out of ignorance has come knowledge and in the process everything is happening. But since the basis is ignorance he does not interfere, because he himself does not know he is. The Jnani cannot focus his attention because he has no attention.

Translator: What Maharaj calls the Knower, the Absolute, gives no attention to anything. Witnessing happens, he doesn't witness. He is beyond that attribute, attention. And you, consciousness, cannot give attention to that. It cannot be known.

Q: Can Maharaj witness his deep sleep state?

M: Oh yes, I witness my deep sleep very nicely.

Q: There was this experience, everything—body and mind—was there, and at the same time, nothing.

M: That is an experience still. The experiencer is different from the experience. Experiences you can describe in thousands of ways, but the experiencer you cannot describe.

Translator: Maharaj says he cannot describe the Absolute, only what appears can he speak about. It cannot be said, "He knows." It is there; it's not a question of knowing.

M: Waking and sleep don't know what was prior to them. Consciousness doesn't know that state, when it was not there. The Absolute knows, but it doesn't belong to the known.

Unknowingly the knowing has started, spontaneously. Once the knowing disappears, then there is nothing. Knowing gives rise to the five elements. When the knowing disappears, you remain. So long as the knowing is there make use of it and inquire. I am stung by a scorpion, what is the stinging? The stinging is this "I Amness." Because you cannot tolerate that sting of "I Amness" you are running from place to place. To nullify the poison of that sting, watch the "I Amness," observe your knowingness. The effect of that sting is the waking state, sleep state, hunger, thirst, etc. Catch hold of that sting, that knowingness.

Q: Is bondage necessary to become free?

M: First you understand what the bondage is. Track yourself down continuously for twenty-four hours. Once you realize "I cannot be a body or a mind," then naturally, you are there.

After all this talk, do you find any necessity for the sound of words? For any talk? Is there any necessity for words? For true spirituality, is there really any need for words?

Q: No.

August 13, 1979

Questioner: The Guru is the greatest power, controlling the outer world as well as the inner. He is more powerful than a king. That's why he is the greatest cheat. He cheats you out of nothing, but you think you lose everything.

Maharaj: If that is your experience, it is quite appropriate. He has appropriated everything, including yourself. That means that you are not a different entity than he. There is no more left of you, only the Guru.

Q: Love makes him the greatest cheat.

M: The love is given to each one according to his needs. If there is no need, can there be love?

Q: From that perspective, no; but the Absolute has always been associated with that concept. Why do we describe It as love?

M: He does not know himself. He does not know what he is. He doesn't need anything. He does not need to call himself "I Am." The Absolute state is called Jnani by ignorant people only. The Absolute doesn't call himself the Absolute or Jnani.

Q: Why have those who are ignorant idealized the Jnani as love?

M: For the ignorant it is a matter of convenience. So long as he has not reached that Jnani state he must have some motive force: to get that, he calls Jnani full of love, compassion, kindness, etc. These are confirmed or imposed by the ignorant.

Q: Is that a correct viewpoint, from an ignorant standpoint?

M: Yes, for the ignorant. There is an idol of Vithobha;

people go and pray to him: "Because of your kindness I survive, etc." The ignorance is talking. Why does the ignorant person keep that stone [idol]? Because he needs to be alive, he wants to perpetuate his "I Amness," to continue. That's why he is worshiping that stone: the need to be.

Q: Isn't it also perhaps one of the ways that the Divine leads the ignorant back to the Absolute?

M: Yes, there are a number of ways or paths for the ignorant.

Q: Wouldn't unconditioned love be faith in form?

M: From my standpoint love is the quality to be. Beingness is love. Only when this "I Amness" appears is there love. Can the love prevail if the "I Amness" is not there? You have the urge to be, to continue your beingness—that is the love.

M: All this manifestation is the ocean of that being. You may call it the ocean of Brahma or the ocean of Maya.

Q: Beyond Maya, beyond the ocean?

M: Where is the question of going beyond? There is beingness-beingness extinguished. It does not go beyond anything. Does it require an airplane, a Boeing, to go somewhere? From where has it come, where did it go? Prior to coming and going, you are.

That "I Amness" is pulsating "I Am-I Am." The feeling of "I Amness" is there because of the essence of the food body and the vital breath. When the food essence and the vital breath are gone, that pulsation of "I Amness" will not be there. Beingness goes into no-beingness.

For the sprouting of any seed, water is necessary. Similarly, for the sprouting of this knowledge "I Am," water and food essence are necessary. In the essence of the food the quality of "I Amness" is in a dormant state. The Atman—the core Self—He himself sees "I Amness" through the juices or essence of the food.

Q: The consciousness is common to all, universal, spontaneous, one. Why does it appear in so many different forms?

M: That is its native quality. Although beingness is one, it manifests in plenty, many, multitudes.

Q: What is satva guna?

M: The quintessence of the food essence is that "I Amness," which is satva guna. Satva guna equals beingness. The beingness is activated in the manifest world through rajas and tamas [gunas]. The rajas is activity. The tamas is the pride you take in doership or authorship. Satva guna is only beingness, just to be. These three gunas have sprung out of the essence of food. If the food is not there that "I Amness" will go, all the qualities will vanish.

Q: That flame of "I Amness" which we see in the present condition with the help of our intellect—it seems that there is a development, a sort of evolution going on. What does Maharaj think—which way is it moving?

M: Toward destruction. Whatever might be the evolution, finally it will be heading toward dissolution.

Turning to what you were speaking about earlier: Is there something you either do or don't want to protect?

Q: I don't know.

M: All this depends on the consciousness, and you don't want to leave the consciousness.

Q: Not even the consciousness of consciousness do I want. I thought of bringing cotton to stuff in my ears when Maharaj is speaking of the Self.

M: Who stays this?

Q: I don't know. Why does it have to be somebody?

M: Who says this?

Q: Words, just words.

M: What is the use of words if consciousness is not there?

Q: Consciousness is there. Why imply that that consciousness does not know?

M: What is the meaning of this? Explain what you have to say.

Q: What is the need of attaching any concept to whatever there is?

M: If you feel "It should be or it should not be," what is there at the bottom of that?

Q: Whatever there is, there is.

M: It is evident that you feel that you are, and therefore it sprouts in you. When you feel that you are, all the trouble starts. If that feeling is not there, no trouble exists.

Q: Why should it give trouble? You attach names and concepts to that which is. Would you leave it alone?

M: Who says this?

Q: Understanding that appears in consciousness.

M: So who is really troublesome? Is the world troubling you, or the consciousness which appears on you?

Q: Nothing troubles me if I shut up.

*M:*That you are sitting there—that itself is going to be troublesome to you. This is your trouble: You are not in a position to sustain that consciousness and you cannot bear it. When the body was not there, when the consciousness was not there, what were you? You are not in a position to understand that.

Q: Before the body was and consciousness appeared, It was whatever It was.

M: Now that you are, you are conscious. Is it because you want it or did it just come automatically, spontaneously to you?

Q: It appears to be spontaneous.

M: You are conscious now, spontaneously, not because you want to be. That's a fact, isn't it?

Q: Yes. I think all this idea of spirituality—of trying to give a meaning to that consciousness—is the only trouble, when consciousness wants to extend itself and be all those things.

M: No, that is not troublesome for you. The troublesome thing is the consciousness appearing on you. It is only because of that that you are giving names or not giving names, doing something or not doing something.

Q: That is the root of the trouble. If consciousness would just be itself and not try to apply concepts to everything, there would be no trouble.

M: This is all imagination.

Q: It is very simple. All the experiences that we call life happen in consciousness, and the meaning of life is just to experience consciousness everywhere. So, when the end comes, then that's it. Cannot consciousness just see and face that end?

M: Can you stay in that?

Q: But what doesn't allow me to stay in that void is looking, searching, trying to do this or that.

M: When the consciousness is there, so is the vital force; thoughts are flowing and a lot of words are coming. That is your mind. Just understand that you are not concerned with the consciousness. It will still be there, it will still continue, but you are not identifying with it, saying, "I am this or I am that."

There should not be any difficulty because the self-evident fact is that you *are*. Why don't you stop there and find out that point? See what that state is.

Translator: Maharaj wants to know if you understand what he is saying to this other person. *You.*

Q: Yes, he is speaking of consciousness.

M: Have you understood the meaning of consciousness?

Q: Consciousness is everything that appears.

M: Who is saying this?

Q: The feeling is, I am.

M: Who experiences this?

Q: Consciousness experiences itself.

M: Yes. Listen to these dialogues for some time more. Whatever is going on, listen for some time more. Thinking "I have understood everything correctly"—that itself is the first mistake. Space is created and thereby the consciousness, which is really non-personal, has become a person, limited to the body and mind. You feel that the consciousness is limited to the body and mind, but if the consciousness is accepted as non-personal, then there is no trouble. Because the knowledge "I Am" is there, we conduct all activities. In the morning when you wake up you get that first guaranty, that conviction of "I Am." Then, because you are not in a position to sustain or tolerate that "I Amness," you bestir your-self. You get up and move around here and there and the activity starts. You involve yourself in all the activity be-cause you want to sustain that "I Amness." Later on that "I Amness' forgets itself in deep sleep; only then are you peaceful.

Q: There is peace in meditation?

M: Why are you going to meditate? To tranquilize the "I Amness." With "I Amness" began all misery. You must spontaneously feel the superficiality of "I Amness."

Q: How?

M: That attention, that "I Amness," is always there in the waking state, but we are not on the alert to watch it. There is no other attention to be followed. Be attentive to that attention "I Am."

Q: Is there something that remains in the deep sleep state?

M: Whatever is there in the waking state merges in the deep sleep and is in a dormant condition.

Q: What is right action?

M: Let the actions happen through you. Don't take yourself to be the doer. There will be actions through you; don't say that these actions are good and those are bad. It is not your responsibility. The one who thinks he is the doer is a slave to mind-inclinations, mind-conditions. The Jnani wit-nesses the consciousness acting; he has no involvement in the actions of the consciousness.

Q: It seems to be an addiction of the consciousness to worry about things around.

M: Yes, addiction, and also entertainment. Suppose I spill water. Immediately I take the towel and wipe it up, but I do not feel that I have done something foolish. It has happened. Just as the towel is soaking up the water without thinking that it is doing so.

Q: What a strange love for this "I Amness."

M: Although it is strange, it gets manifested in concrete forms. We all hang on to concepts about saving the world, doing good. With all the great concepts and ideas great people have had, where are the saved and the saviors today? What do you over there want?

Q: I would like everything to be in harmony, non-chaotic.

M: Don't hang on to name and form. Get rid of name and form.

Q: Why is it so difficult to understand that simple thing?

M: Because whatever you have understood, you are clinging to, embracing. Get rid of that. Whatever you have understood from this world, you are hanging onto. Give it up. The way that you understand yourself, give that up also.

August 14, 1979

Maharaj: How many years were you with your Guru?

Questioner: Nearly six years.

M: What was the purpose of his Jnana, Yoga, whatever it may have been?

Q: He teaches that humanity is ready to take a big step in consciousness. An era of enlightenment can be created now. Until now all the sages, saints and saviors that the world has had have been working on ideas. Ideas cannot make that change, but if a small portion of humanity raises its consciousness level through the type of meditation that he has provided, the effect will be a higher level of consciousness generally.

M: The whole consciousness is already there, so what are you going to change? How are you going to change?

Q: But it is a fact that a change in consciousness can take place in any particular form.

M: Yes, it can be changed, but it cannot remain permanent.

Q: All right, it cannot be made permanent; but is that a reason why that improvement in consciousness should not be made?

M: You can change it for the better, but who is to enjoy that?

Q: That is a very important point to clear, a difficult point, you know. We know the world is going to explode into pieces, and some people say, let it destroy itself, it is impermanent. People won't allow that such a change in consciousness can take place now.

M: That which is spontaneous, that which has come without any reason, how are you going to stop it? Who has made this whole thing? Find out from where this talk is emanating. What is the source? The source is the little touch of "I Amness," that pinprick which has no dimension. But just see what a manifestation it has created, how that talk is flowing out, but from where? From that little pinprick, that dimensionless touch of "I Amness."

You are angry with me and you feel it. What will happen? You can't kill me. I will increase, more and more, a millionfold I will increase. I am speaking from that angle. Can you destroy me? Whatever is dead, you see, is the food of this illusion, the mind. It can absorb any number of deaths. It never dies. Maya will still be there.

Q: It is astonishing to us that Maharaj doesn't seem to have love for this "I Amness." He seems to be somewhere else, not involved in it.

M: You mean to say that I should love that trouble? What will happen if I love that self? I will suffer more pain, or I will get more money. What's the use of that?

Translator: Maharaj says, if you bring more and more money and give it to him, what will happen? There will be a monument—beautiful stones, decorated and worshiped. That is of no use to him.

Q: Maybe not for him, but that might be useful for somebody else.

M: It will be useful only for other human beings, that's all.

Q: Where did Maharaj find the courage to stand completely alone?

M: Who requires courage? It is your nature. Why should I bother about this body? Just last night twenty-five thousand people died in Gujarat, in just one night. Why should I bother about this body here?

I had faith, devotion, so many things. This consciousness, this pinprick, I know its complete nature. Nothing remains, no faith, no devotion, nothing at all. Whatever I used to have in those days, all is gone.

Translator: The "I" that met his Guru and the "I" speaking now are two different levels.

Q: What is the use of the manifested world then?

M: There is no question of use or no use. That is the nature of consciousness, in which the world appears. The world has a use for one who considers himself the body. Through your senses the world appears to be real, but it is only temporary, for a short duration. It is just like a sickness, when you are feeling sick. It's the sickness of that illusion, Maya.

Q: We are incarnated in a body; then how can we not be the body?

M: If you consider yourself to be a body, you have more to lose than to gain. If you don't consider yourself the body, then what can you say you are?

Q: But if you cut my leg I scream.

[Maharaj bangs the ashtray on the metal container, which produces a loud PING.]

M: Look, this also feels the pain, it is shouting also—now it is quiet! You are wrongly identifying yourself with the body. You are not that. It is for you to realize it.

Q: There are sometimes glimpses, when I don't feel the body, and there is no time—it is timeless.

M: Right. Although most of the time you are identifying with the body, if even for a short while you feel you are not the body, that's enough. Out of ignorance the knowledge "I Am" comes into being; and into ignorance, where it doesn't know itself, it will dissolve again. After understanding this you can go, and whatever you do doesn't matter; it's all God's doing. You are not the doer anymore, you never were. When the television set is burned or destroyed, will the people in the movie feel the pain and die? You have no form, no shape, you are like the sky. The vital breath which you take in—will it feel any pain when you die? It will just merge into the air again, as it was before.

But just to sit here and listen will not do. You have to meditate.

August 15, 1979

Maharaj: During the state of beingness there are two main states, waking and sleep. What was before these states? Are you born, or is it the waking and sleep states that are born? The waking state is the reminder that "I Am," and deep sleep is forgetting "I Amness." What else is there except the birth of these two states? Why don't you talk on this, these states of memory and no-memory? If these are not there, what is it you want? For acquisition of which knowledge have you come here? If you agree with what I say, why do you want to come here tomorrow? To get what?

Questioner: I don't want to gain or acquire; I want to lose. I want to get rid of this realm of concepts.

M: If these two states are not there, could there be concepts?

Q: Without waking and sleep states what remains?

M: Whatever That is—without memory and no-memory—That remains. The waking and sleep states are impermanent. It is all the greatness of that chemical, that great Spirit. Out of that principle these states and this manifestation, this world, comes.

You are not the deep sleep and waking states, and without these you are not. Wherever you may roam, this talk will occur to you again and again.

In the womb this "I Amness" in the form of ignorance is there. The child is born and after a couple of years that ignorance becomes knowledgeable—"I Am." Before understanding this "I Amness," there is Balakrishna, the child ignorance. Later on it understands itself—that is knowledge. This knowledge cancels out the Balakrishna ignorance. In this Krishna state, Lord Krishna expounded the knowledge, and after that he merged in his original state, the Absolute.

So long as that ignorance-knowledge is given, each cancels the other. Like this flame, so long as that ignorance is there, that flame of knowledge will be there. When that ignorance is exhausted, finished, that flame of knowledge will also be finished.

Who directed you to this place?

Q: Anandamayi, Krishnabai, and some friends at Sri Ramanasram.

M: What is your native place?

Q: We are both from France.

M: Having performed all this physical and mental discipline, what is it that you want to be?

Q: My own Self.

M: Has your Guru indicated what your Self is?

Q: It is something which is already there and we have to find it out.

M: Who is to search for it?

Q: I have to remove all the obstacles which prevent me from really living in the present.

M: Who is going to remove the obstacles?

Q: I am.

M: Who are you?

Q: There is an element of consciousness which is trying to find out.

M: This consciousness—who told you about consciousness?

Q: I have been longing for this path, there is something which drives one, leads one to this path.

M: Why do you get entangled in words? You know that

you are. No one has to tell you that you exist, you know it automatically.

Q: Obstacles prevent this consciousness. . . .

M: Let us deal with these obstacles [samskaras] later. Deal with the Self, the knowledge "I Am." This "I Amness" is there first, isn't it?—primary. That "I" must be there first before you receive this sickness of samskara. How long will you be in Bombay?

Q: Just five more days.

M: If you are already in the queue and get the number for this spiritual knowledge, then any amount of obstacles will be brushed aside. But if you are not in that line, you will be roaming about. Initially you have to understand that the knowledge "I Am" is the product of the food essence. When you know that you are, the world also is.

As salt is in seawater, similarly, in the body, in combination with the vital breath, the consciousness appears. It is the consciousness that feels pain or pleasure, not the body or the vital breath. Once you know that you are not the body, all the concepts about pain and pleasure will disappear by themselves. Are you convinced that this is true?

Q: Yes.

M: Here you get the knowledge of what you are, now you have to experience it yourself. To keep quiet and watch for yourself is called meditation. Remaining in what you have heard here is called spiritual practice.

The Guru, God, your own knowledge—these three are one. If you know that, you become quiet. Guru means knowledge and knowledge means "I Am." "I Amness' is itself the Guru.

August 16, 1979

Maharaj: When people go about on their search for spiritual knowledge they don't think for themselves. They only think of what knowledge [concepts] they have already acquired.

Many who come here have read *I Am That*. They come here to see, as a curiosity, who this person is. They have a look and then go away. If you want to find out something more, then sit quietly and listen for as long as you can, and try to understand what is said.

What is to be understood, have you understood?

Questioner: I have difficulties accepting. I watch this incredible resistance building up.

M: Who says that?

Q: The difficulty itself.

M: Whatever is to be understood is there, One. That state in which you were before you acquired this knowledge "I Am" is the real state. Only after you got this knowledge you identified with the body-mind. Whatever you have acquired, including the body-mind, that will go, and it is useless, and that is that. But your original state, before you acquired the body, is the Truth, is the Real state, and it will remain.

Infancy has grown into youth, middle age, and old age. During all these stages, that enjoyment you had of being, of being alive, of existing, all that is false. All these stages will disappear, and that which understands, even that will go.

Q: Concerning this coming and going that Maharaj talks about—are they experiences of the body or of consciousness?

M: Through what do you derive experiences?

Q: Through the senses.

M: What is the original cause of your existence, what is it a mixture of?

Q: My existence is this consciousness, and all the happenings are already contained in consciousness.

I don't agree that you can lose it, as you say. The body may go, but all the experiences in consciousness, consciousness itself, don't go. What goes is the particular form of this body, but the knowing, which is consciousness itself, doesn't go. That will appear again in another form.

M: How did you get your form? What is the cause of that form?

Q: That is another matter.

M: No second and no third and not another. I am talking to *you.* It concerns *you.* I am asking *you* about that first moment of mix-up. This body, this form is there. What is the root cause?

Q: Two people getting together. These two people getting together, is it not that same knowing prolonging itself? Consciousness itself keeping this movement. . . .

M: I want to know the name and form of that mixture.

Q: All name and all form.

M: You are not hearing what I am talking about. It is not reaching you. Keep quiet.

Do you understand the cause of your calling some person your parent? Is it by the bodies or the essences of the bodies?

Q: The essences.

M: What exactly has happened there?

Q: I don't know.

M: You presume you have become a Jnani and are going to write a book, don't you?

Q: No, he is presuming that I am going to write a book. Because I am seeing a Jnani, that's why I am in this discussion.

M: In that state in which the mind was not—put your attention there. Pay attention to that state.

You are all just like people who visit many shops, spiritual shops. To get a taste of various delicacies, tasting bit by bit, little by little.

Q: If Maharaj has answered all his questions, why are all these questions coming through his mind?

M: I am apart from the questions.

Q: It is no solution, talking.

M: It appears to you like that? Pay attention and it will happen. You must learn to live without identifying yourself with the body. All activities, even the mind flow, come from the vital breath. Give attention to the consciousness—that is meditation.

Q: Thoughts grab us and take us away.

M: Thoughts have so much power because of the identification with the body.

Q: It is very difficult just to watch pain. I become afraid.

M: What is watching pain is yourself. With consciousness you have to hold consciousness. Give attention to this "I" taste. Don't give attention to fear, give attention to what you are. Once you know what you are you become fearless. Remove the concept of death from your mind. There is no death as such. I am sure you are not going to die. That is only a concept or idea.

Your identification with the body has continued since childhood, so in order to get rid of it also takes time.

For the beingness to sustain itself there is occupation. Whatever you gain has no value, and the one who gains also has no value. You will come to understand the hollowness of this game. Only in your ignorant phase you take everything as so important. We give undue importance to things that come and go.

I am talking from the standpoint where I do not know of myself, that I am. I don't belong to the realm of waking and sleep states. How can I presume that I am like this or that? You presume that I am something or somebody.

Q: Could Maharaj talk about posture, Hatha Yoga, a little bit?

M: I don't deal with any physical disciplines, nor with Yoga, nor with anything you get from it. What I am trying to expound is this: you are I only, I am you. I know that you are I only, but you don't know; so I am trying to give you that introduction, that acquaintance. By performing these physical Yoga asanas, etc., you get a certain satisfaction, but that is not spiritual knowledge.

Q: Do people acquire powers through the Yoga process?

M: In the Yogic process some people acquire powers, but it does have an end. It is not the Ultimate, the Eternal. This Absolute, this Eternal, people do not get instantly. People get involved in powers and miracles and revel in that only. They will be busy with that but not the Ultimate. They will undergo rebirths.

August 17, 1979

Maharaj: The experience of consciousness comes through the body, and when you start looking at the body, it is nothing but food.

Questioner: There are so many propensities in me—the propensities of food, of the senses, of attachment, of thinking—call it anything you like. I hear Maharaj as a sort of intellectualized music, something which is not intellect, but the music that comes out of the intellect. How can I ignore that? I can't ignore it, it is there all the time. I know that everything has come out of the food, but what is before me is not food; it is just like a flower.

M: What is it that has these propensities?

Q: As an integrated, social self I hear the music. How can I ignore that?

M: What is that principle which is the substratum for all these experiences? You must find that out.

The moment you awaken from sleep you seem to know the whole world. This passing show, which is in a state of flux the whole time, is thrown like a picture on your beingness. Through an illusion we are thinking that "I" have a separate personality, that "I" am a separate self. The consciousness which is all-pervading does not have this feeling of limited beingness. This all-pervading consciousness has no ignorance and no knowledge, but ignorance and knowledge take birth in it.

When I ignite the cigarette lighter you say that the flame is, when I put it out you say that the flame is not; so also the flame of knowledge is and is not.

Until such time as your words have stopped, there is meaning in the words, and there is nothing in the meaning also. The meaning is itself meaningless.

Q: If the words are meaningless how should we listen to you?

M: Don't listen to me, you listen to your own Self and find out how much you are in your own company.

Q: We do not know how to be with our own Self. It is so ugly we always run away from it.

M: But you are caught up in it. Even if you call yourself ugly and do not like your own company, can you decide to take your food out of it and leave it?

The seed that is sown is so small, and yet so many flowers, fruits, the tree trunk, and everything has come out of it. I eat all that, and I eat the seed, and the seed is for my strength and contentment and satisfaction. When I become my Self I understand that beingness is with me.

So many desires, so many dreams, come on this body which knows "I am." That beingness has taken hold of this five elemental body. You must find out what is sustaining itself on the body which is its food.

Birth and death are only terms, names. When death has come it only means that the experience called birth is extinguished.

Q: When we hear Maharaj an idea comes into the mind that death is wonderful and it can come soon and be forever.

M: When the death is forever it means that Eternal Immutable Parabrahman.

Q: Besides listening to Maharaj, is there any other tablet to invite death?

M: If you decide, finally, that you are not this body, the death will be final; death will die. Therefore try just to live without this consciousness of body and mind.

The body is dependent on the essence of food. The food is dependent on the five elements, and the five elements are the life of that one which has no name. If you try to find out your beingness—that source from which you have come—there will be no name, no form, and no identity of your own.

Q: I am trying a new experiment. Whatever I am, I don't need to describe it, nor name it, nor question anything. Whatever I am, I am, and that's it. Not looking at whatever is as separate from me, but just to be.

M: If you can manage that, then by all means do. If you get peace and can understand the Truth that way, that is very good.

August 18, 1979

Questioner: Why is the understanding so fleeting, changing?

Maharaj: It depends on the body sense. All people will receive the knowledge from here, but the behavior of each will be different from that of the others.

Q: Myself, I am holding on to the same consciousness, and the understanding which is reflected in that consciousness is changing completely from day to day.

M: Oh yes. This knowledge, "I Am," in the field of mind-inclination, mind-understanding, will not remain the same. It is changing every moment. It will never stabilize itself on one understanding.

Q: So there is no such thing as final understanding?

M: The beginning and the end of this understanding is the knowledge "I Am." The beginning of concepts started with the primary concept "I Am." Having wandered through all the concepts and rejected them, you have to get rid of this last or the first concept.

Q: That rejection—does it come by the disappearing of the last concept, just by giving it attention?

M: See this flame of the cigarette lighter? It has appeared, it has disappeared; it's just like that. Has it got any concept, this flame? What is without concept is the most perfect, the most proper. The witnessing has to be done when you try to concentrate on an objective. Suppose you want to concentrate on a Rama, a Krishna, or a Christ, then there is a question of concentrating or watching. This is only the knowledge "I Am."

Q: The problem is, the more attention I give to consciousness, the larger the concept which appears in the mind.

M: How do you focus attention on consciousness? Consciousness itself has to focus.

Q: That is what I meant.

M: Understand consciousness and come to the conclusion that consciousness is not yourself.

Q: I can't. I *cannot!*

M: Give it up! Whatever demands you make, I am not going to fulfill. I am not going to meet your demands. I am not going to give you whatever you want. I am just going to tell you, to emphasize what you are. You want to convert or transform yourself into something: "I want to become this," "I am going to do that." I am going to tell you what is the root of you, the innermost core, what you are. I am not a sculptor, you see, I don't make images for you, so that you become that image.

Q: Where does this need of consciousness to see itself as everything come from?

M: You know that you are, and you love to be, hence the necessity. Although you have been saying that you understood, there is some hitch somewhere, isn't there?

Q: One card. I am holding back one card.

M: Throw it out! Where is the loss? Give up the game. You listen to my talks or don't listen. You come here or don't come here. I know what you are, what you were prior to your "I Amness." Before your parents met, I know you. I know your knowingness after your parents met, how it got transformed to various stages, how it developed in different images, I know all that. Suppose a person is a hundred twenty-five years old; since childhood he has grown into various stages, learned a lot worldly things. Now whatever he has learned or gained, everything has gone, and he is lying on a bed, and what remains now? Only that child-consciousness, that child-ignorance, remains. And that also will go. Will it go to heaven or hell? No; the ignorance has sprung up and the ignorance will disappear.

Q: The question then is, if that ignorance can disappear

only through that process of time or can it be stopped now?

M: Even in between. It is sustained by food and water. If this is not supplied it will go, disappear.

Q: But it has gone in the case of Maharaj and there is a supply of food and water there. So what I am asking is, is that process inevitable, or can it just end now?

M: You have to meditate. It won't be available free. The necessary threshold is through consciousness only. You have to imbibe and be consciousness. In the process of being in the consciousness, you come out of it, and there you see; and meditation is the only remedy.

Q: The more you get into consciousness, the more impossible it seems to transcend it.

M: Give it a fair trial. Be in beingness. Try to be in beingness. You won't get it here and now. Step number one is: Be yourself, be in your beingness only. Although, to start with, I am the Immanent Spirit "I Am," you have to be in that beingness without the body sense. You feel that you are the body now, but when you abide in that beingness you will know then how you are without the body. But don't forget, at the same time, that body and vital breath are very necessary. Once you understand these three entities correctly [body, vital breath and the message "I Am"], then you are apart. The knower of these three entities will not be caught by the parents.

Q: When Maharaj was immersed in his beingness, what exactly did he understand that made him transcend consciousness?

M: You know TV? Meditate and you will know as tangibly as you see TV. You will see then: I am not the TV screen, the observer of TV is not in the set. In the process of meditation, more knowledge will be awakened, will be realized by you, and, in the same process, you will understand that whatever you have understood you are not.

Q: That's why I was saying before that the more consciousness was conscious of itself, the larger the concept, the knowledge.

M: Yes, it will happen, a living cosmos, a million universes are in your consciousness.

Q: What about the knower?

M: The knower and whatever is known, both will go. Nothing will remain stable, permanent. This triangle, father, mother, and you, how did it happen? Inquire about that, meditate on that.

Q: Isn't it the same thing, father, mother, and I; just a flow of that consciousness?

M: Don't talk, try to understand. Just talking about eating will not fill your stomach, you have to actually eat. You will not get eternal peace with knowledge derived out of words, only by Self-knowledge, Self-realization.

August 19, 1979

Questioner: How can I achieve what Maharaj speaks about?

Maharaj: Remember your beingness. The knowledge that "I Am" has come to you out of your satva guna; that is beingness. Satva, rajas, and tamas: three gunas are playing here in the manifestation. The quality of the satva, the essence, is to know that you are, and to provide you with that basis on which to act. Rajas is the motivating factor, it makes you move about, and tamas is inertia, consolidation. This knowledge "I Am" comes to you after your body is born; after that the body of childhood grows on its own and becomes old. What is left after all the ambitions, all the desires, have been fulfilled, all the actions have been done in accordance with the natural disposition?

What remains in the end is only one thing, "I Am." So all through life you have to remember to investigate who is this "I Am"; otherwise birth and death will have no meaning for your beingness, because that beingness also will be dissolved after the death of the body.

Q: Beingness will be dissolved after the death of the body?

M: This beingness is the quality of the essence of the food body. Actually, that beingness is living on the food that is your body. All bodies are food. That feeling of beingness appears in the body and is dissolved when the body drops off.

Beingness means loving that feeling of self. Love is included in the beingness and that love grows as the body grows. For more and more love to be given to that beingness, so much manifestation, so many other things are required in order to satisfy that love. "This I want for that comfort," comfort of the body and that beingness, the love to be. In order to satisfy that craving you must have a wife, you must have a house, you must have clothes and other comforts, and this goes on. This beingness only creates karma. Actually, nobody is born and nobody dies. The fact is that beingness appears and beingness disappears.

Q: How could karma act from life to life, and what about God?

M: The one who understands the meaning of the word God is himself God.

Q: What remains after the knowledge of beingness dissolves?

M: See, the cigarette lighter is lit, now it is extinguished, but does it mean that it is dead? That beingness, when extinguished, is dissolved into Brahman, from where it came.

Q: If beingness is dissolved then there is no karma?

M: If that beingness is not there, can there be actions? When the beingness is there the manifestation is there, and the actions happen in the realm of that consciousness. There is no doer. We erroneously claim to be the doer.

That "I Amness" is like a seed of the berry. In that berry seed all the forest of berry trees is already present in potential condition. Likewise, this "I Amness" is the seed of manifestation in which actions happen, and there is no doer. How is the seed formed in a fruit? Out of the essence of the juice of that fruit the seed is formed. What does it mean when the seed is formed? It is recording all the images of the formation of the tree already recorded in the tree itself, which will again, in due course, proliferate into another tree, but all this is recorded in the seed only. The same thing applies to the human seed. When the seed is planted, when does it record the image of the parents, so that that particular seed assumes the image of the father or mother, gets a particular body form? What is the principle?

Take for example the TV screen. On the screen you see all the images acting. These images are already recorded somewhere and are being played now. So, they will not stop even if we shout and ask them to. That is one not very good example. The human or natural seed recording out of which the same or similar images grow is spontaneous, while the TV recording is out of the skill of the human intellect.

Q: In the Buddhist teaching there is not a full solution. There are remaining aggregates that will form a new being.

M: Whatever Buddha's philosophy is, these are all various ideas, various concepts. In each person the ideas are sprouting and when they spontaneously come out, he behaves accordingly. He follows those ideas because he likes them, they have come out of him.

I am not inclined to follow various ideas or the judgment of others. Among the judgments, the best is given by Lord Krishna. He says we have to get out of our own judgment, our own concepts about ourself. Do not depend on anybody else.

Now you listen to these talks and realize your own ultimate position. Your true position, which you will not lose again. You stabilize there. My Guru also indicated to me my ultimate destination and I have stabilized myself in it.

It occurs to one's attention that one is. When it was not in the attention of that one, was the principle not there? It was. That principle is unblemished and without attention. In non-attention it prevails. Eternally.

And what does it mean—whatever acquired is surrendered in oblations to the Brahman? All this knowledge, this knowingness, is offered to Brahman.

Q: If the body is food for beingness, we shall feel insecure for the body. It will not be peace, quietness, because we shall be anxious for the beingness, through the body.

M: When you leave your body who is the customer for that peace?

Q: Even if I am not identified with the body, but I know that it is food for the beingness, I feel anxious.

M: It is good that you are careful and anxious to preserve the body, but remember that this manifested body is dependent on the essence of the food that you eat.

Out of the essences or juices of vegetation all species are formed: insects, animals, human beings, etc. This quality of beingness is in the juices, the vegetation, in a dormant condition. In each species that knowingness is there. The principle—just to know. It is not a question of whose knowingness, only beingness or knowingness is there.

Q: Are there different kinds of beingness?

M: The expression of consciousness through different bodies is different. The body shape is different, the voice is different, ideas are different, sound is different, tastes are different. It is infinitely varied.

Q: How can the beingness be different? Beingness is only one.

M: Sound as such is the same, but its expression through different instruments is different. Out of the same consciousness, with the formation of a Krishna body a Krishna is born; a donkey also is formed accordingly. Consciousness is the same.

Q: Are the gunas dependent on the food you eat, or are they already there?

M: In the initial stage, it is all right for you to understand that everything potentially is this food value. You start with this food value and vital breath, this combination and that "I Amness"; but later on, you have to investigate and understand how this "I Amness" has come. You have to go to the root, root means mula, mula means a child. How has that child formation taken place? In the process, when you go to the source itself, you will realize that "I Amness" contains this manifested universe, like a seed. To understand more clearly, take the example of the dream world. You are in deep sleep and suddenly you feel "I Am," and that "I Amness" creates a dream world. Similarly this manifest world is created by that "I Amness." You will realize this later in the search for the truth. The last progress will be for you to transcend this "I Amness" also and get stabilized in the Ultimate.

Don't presume that having understood all this word-ly knowledge you are full of wisdom. To think that will be something like being severely constipated. Whatever I have expounded to you is to be realized by the Self.

Before this beingness came to you, you were all the time there, but you were not conscious of it. The Absolute doesn't know Itself at all. Our true state is not of knowledge, but prior to knowledge.

August 20, 1979

Questioner: Your philosophy starts where science ends. I have myself learned a lot in the field of medicine and elsewhere, but after reading your book I have humbled myself at your feet. Who is the one you call Atman? Who is the knower and where is he situated in the body? If there is some injury or wound to the toe, you understand it, but from where does this understanding come? From the neck to the head, there is somebody who knows. Where is that knowledge situated?

Maharaj: It is in the Brahma-randhra [opening in the crown of the head]. Some Yogis collect all their vital breath there and steady themselves, but they do not understand the fundamental principle.

A great man performed severe penance for a long time; in the end a vision appeared before him. The great man was very dirty, so he said to the vision, "I will clean myself and then meet you." When the man appeared completely clean the vision ate him up. They became one, one beauty, bliss, and joy. All that you are experiencing now is what is to be discarded as dirty, and in what is to be discarded that one knowledge, beingness, is existing.

Q: What does this mean?

M: That portion of the body below the neck is full of the stench of sour food, but it is in this body that the secret soul is living: it doesn't get dirty. That one lives here and his life, his sensitivity, or knowledge, has spread all through the body. It gives you everything that is beautiful, everything that is fragrant. Your existence is all-pervading. All the four Vedas do not know how to praise you.

In the drop of "I Amness" all the universe is contained. Since you understand the drop, can you be the drop? "I Amness" indicates the Parabrahman, but it is not the Parabrahman.

Q: Is the consciousness real or unreal?

M: It is a dreaming consciousness. You are unreal, therefore the world is unreal. It is an illusion, Maya.

Q: Why is the illusion, Maya, creating all these embodied lives?

M: The farmer produces grain in order to eat it, and Maya produces life in order to eat it. Maya doesn't live on life but on the death of that life, because without these forms it cannot function.

Q: According to scientists matter cannot be destroyed; it always gets transformed from one state to another.

M: What is that state where there is no change, that immutable condition? The homogeneous state in which there is no "I" and no "you"—nothing is there; only that is the eternal truth. What is your real nature? How do you identify yourself? If you identify with the body, along with the body you will die.

Q: I am trying to break this identity with the ego.

M: To feel that you are an individual is itself a conditioning; the one who wants to break the conditioning is also imaginary. How can you destroy an ego which is not there? The knowledge "I Am" is the first ignorance and whatever knowledge you acquire with it is ignorance. Go back to the source of your ignorance.

With half knowledge we think we are full of wisdom, profound; that is our presumption. When we are without thoughts, then only are we profound. Realize the thought-free state. Don't worry about other people and other things. Do your own research, try to find out how you happen to be.

The principle which understands—its language is the mind. In the end, both whatever is understood and the one who understands are liquidated. Many people have understood and they have gone into quietude.

August 21, 1979

Maharaj: Consciousness is everywhere, latent or otherwise. First there is consciousness, then came everything, the sky, the earth, and all.

Questioner: This consciousness, it is not the same as the "I Am," the Self consciousness, is it?

M: Whenever we think of consciousness we think of the body, but that is an error. The original state was there before the waking and sleep states.

Q: The "I Am" dissolves after death, so it is not the same.

M: Are you speaking now of the individual personality or the universal consciousness?

Q: The universal Self.

M: The consciousness that prevails is the universal consciousness. The world is born out of that, and not from the point of view of the individual personality.

Q: What is the relationship between the universal consciousness and the "I Amness"?

M: The spark of the incense stick and the whole of it—that is the relationship. That consciousness which prevails before you are aware of the two states is the universal consciousness. You will not learn this through your thoughts, but when you meditate, that consciousness of being will merge into universal consciousness, and only in that way will you understand it. The universal consciousness has always been, its power always present. Its power of creation has given rise to this world, it has produced this Prakriti and Purusa, and its soul is the individual consciousness.

It is spontaneous, manifest, dynamic Spirit. It has no aspect. It is all-pervading. I am talking about that Vedic principle, Vedic raw material, out of which this flow has started. That universal life force pervades everything, but it has no personality or individuality.

Q: How does one witness the thoughts, the concepts?

M: It goes on automatically. You are always aware of those concepts and thoughts.

Q: I know it after, but not during.

M: If you suddenly want to go some place, you get up and go. You know that, so what is the question of another witness? You were sitting for meditation this morning, and when the bhajans started you got up and left. That walking out happened, didn't it? Do you want any other dimension to witness it?

Q: Again the same question: can we be a witness of our own minds?

M: In the morning your mind directed you to leave and you walked off. Is it not witnessing?

Q: Yes, I can witness one movement, but I cannot be witness to my thought during the thought process.

M: The consciousness is acting as a whole, no doer is there. We look at ourselves as doers, and therefore we want to witness it, which cannot be done. Therefore you abide in the words of the Guru, which are: You are the all-pervading subtle principle, subtler than space. Identify yourself with that.

Q: A person wants to attain peace through meditation, samadhi, etc., but it is a temporary peace, because, as you say, it is a product of the body. How is one to get eternal peace?

M: You witness that peace, so there is peace and the witness. Be there. In due course both this peace and the witness will go. What remains is the Absolute. This is very subtle, the last stage. There is nothing tangible there to understand with the gross senses. This is only to be experienced.

After listening to these talks you leave this place and tell people, "For God's sake, don't go there! My head is full of turmoil, it is all confusion. Whatever sense I had, whatever understanding I had, it is all gone!"

Q: Some people do witness their past lives. How is that?

M: That's because they believe it. Just like the promises of politicians, it is all talk.

Q: The Tibetans choose their Lama because he is a reincarnation.

M: It is a traditional concept and we do not take any note of such concepts. If you want any reply, we will become whatever concept we entertain at the time of death. It will take concrete shape according to the concept.

Q: If I have the concept of God at the time of death, will I become God?

M: But you must also have a concept of what kind of God! Four-armed, three-headed or ten-headed!

The trouble is, all of you want to derive some benefit from your concepts and ideas. Don't employ any thoughts for your use. Without recourse to thought, understand and remain.

It is not possible for people of ordinary needs or intellect to come here. It must be an evolved soul who can think of coming here. This one comes daily. Do you think it is an individual's need or a body's need? No. It means that the soul wants to return to its source. The great saint Tukaram said, "I want to return to my mother's home."

Q: Someone was telling me of an experience he had after visiting Maharaj. . . .

M: Some people who have visited here have had certain experiences, and they call Maharaj "great," etc. Whom are they calling great? I am nothing, I am completely void.

Q: How is one to get out of this vicious circle?

M: You are caught in this vortex; if you want to escape you must go to the center. Dive deep inside. This vicious circle of life, death, rebirth, etc., started with consciousness. Try to understand that consciousness, and in the process of understanding, you will become its background, the basis.

August 22, 1979

Questioner: I can see that unless there is a center within me I cannot conduct myself. After attaining that center, unfortunately for my life, a psychological condition appeared. In my body there are certain sensitivities, certain throbbings going on which give me pleasant or unpleasant sensations. I would like to know why they are there.

Maharaj: These sensations arise because the five elements have created duality. Duality also means a sort of chaos and disagreement, so wherever there are elements there will be a quarrel among them; therefore they give you these pleasant or unpleasant sensations. Whatever we eat gives us the experiences we call pleasant or unpleasant. Whatever agreement or disagreement there is among the five elements has to be endured by everyone.

The Vedas have told you the way of behavior: It is very necessary for a person to understand these scriptures, because they provide some kind of path, how to behave, how to conduct yourself.

It is so wonderful, so amazing, that that essence, through you, has taken the form "I know," and consciousness has appeared in this body in the form "I Am"; and following that consciousness a big account has also been opened up.

Q: How does Maharaj look upon us?

M: I am the knower of the universal life and I look upon you also as one like me, but I know that you do not know what you are. I understand from what platform you are talking, and what your nature is I also know.

If you become a Jnani you sort of feel proud: "I" have acquired this, "I" have done this—but it is not going to last. All life is universal life, it has nothing to do with an individual. There is no sense in taking pride in whatever "I" know or "I" have done in life.

Q: Is what Maharaj calls the sense the same as intelligence?

M: It is all this One, but whatever is here is made impure by gunas: that is the state of beingness, the knowledge "I Am."

Q: Isn't there some direction for that intelligence from inside?

M: Inside of what? What are you directing your attention to?

Q: Toward the human body. One experiences this sense, or this intelligence, and at the same time experiences many things which appear false, which are still in the form of elements. It creates so many problems. How does one act on it?

M: That particle from which this birth has come includes crores of elements. Close your eyes and you will see: it is the seed of the whole universe, the smallest, the atomic, and yet it contains crores of universes within the seed.

Q: Have we just to live with them and not do anything about them? Can we not act on the potentialities?

M: With what are you going to act? Before eating food you can do anything with it, but once it goes into the stomach, what can you do with it? That consciousness is doing whatever is being done to the food. What are you doing? Try the experiment in the dream world.

Q: No, I don't have any dream world. I am thinking of myself, the elements which are in me, in this body; I am acting from that.

M: For the sake of that, many births will come. You are not the body, you do not have a personality, you are the universal life. This is all universal life. Why do you consider yourself some particular individual and suffer?

August 23, 1979

Maharaj: How long have you been wearing this garb [ocher robes]?

Questioner: Twenty-five years.

M: Have you realized your Self?

Q: I am not realized. I am just wandering about, as you say, in the dark jungle, going here and there.

M: Who is it that says this?

Q: Probably the Self.

M: Remember that whatever is called God or Self is in the body, and as long as He is there, that beingness will be also. When beingness is not there, there will be no God, no Self. When a person dies it is not the Self that is turned into a corpse, it is the body.

Q: It is true. You see, I understand all that theoretically, I know it as a philosophy, but to experience the void, to know the Real, I am as far off as possible.

M: Whatever is called God or Self is because there is the beingness, the feeling that "I Am." That is the fundamental principle, the basis behind all your knowledge, but you are identifying yourself with the body.

Q: True.

M: When there is no soul there is no God, and when you are not there, your feeling of beingness is not there, there is nothing.

Q: I understand the theory of it. I have read so many books. But how to realize it?

M: When you understand the meaning of the words, you must find out who it is that understands.

Q: You see, that is the gap, to know is very difficult.

M: That which is going to turn into a corpse—you are calling that "me," "I." This is the sin that you are committing and the obstacle between you and the knowledge.

Q: That is the difference; that gap needs to be bridged.

M: All these words are absolutely unnecessary. Because you are, there is the light, the light of knowledge, and when

you are gone the light of knowledge will be extinguished.
Did not your Guru tell you this?

Q: It's just like saying that this candy is sweet, do you get
the taste of it?

M: Has not your Guru told you whatever you are hearing
now?

Q: Yes, yes.

M: That means that you do not agree with him. You still
have not trusted him.

Q: I agree, I trust, but maybe I am lacking in effort.

M: You are lacking in nothing! You have understood
yourself as a corpse, a body. Are you that which is going to
be extinguished?

Q: I know I am not.

M: Then what kind of sadhana are you going to perform? If you are not that which is going to be extinguished,
you are not going to die.

Q: I understand that position—it is not that I don't
understand.

M: Why are you traveling around then?

Q: I am looking for something. I am trying to find something I have not been able to find.

M: You say that you understand and yet you say that
you don't get it; so, are you telling a lie?

Q: I don't know myself. You see, for me, it is all there, I
know you don't have to go about. You sit in one place, in
your own home, and you find it out; but *I* have yet to find it.
So the thought comes to go around, that impatience to find
out which drives one from place to place, till one finds something. Well, I haven't found it. The day I find it, then I also
will say, "Yes, it is within."

M: When you close your eyes, inside you see Ganesan
[darkness] with the feeling "I Am," and when you open your
eyes, the same shows you what is outside. You do not have
to think to perform that act. All has appeared without your
active contribution.

Q: That is the philosophy of it, but doing it is the difficult part, very difficult.

M: Why are you not taking delivery of that fact? What

is the use of wandering from place to place? You are defaming the ocher robes.

Q: True.

M: You see, your soul is so wonderful, so great, and so important that if you sit in a barren land, it will be filled with beautiful gardens. You do not understand your own greatness, the knowledge that you are, your beingness.

Q: No, I am not great. I am very humble, very small.

M: What is humble and what is small? What is there without your beingness? Even if you perform great penances, you can, at the most, punish your body. Can you punish your beingness?

Q: No.

M: When they send a man to the gallows, can they hang his soul, his beingness? This body is hanged. Can you possibly punish the beingness?

Q: No.

M: So He is not humble or small. He enjoys all the wonderful qualities, but He is absolutely unattached, not smeared by any of them. You see, your attire is showing you have that. We don't wear such attire. Nobody will call me a Mahatma.

Q: I am not a Mahatma.

M: Then why are you wearing these robes? You don't worry about what you are telling others by wearing such robes, but you enjoy feeling "I am the great Mahatma, I am the greatest of all." Because you know and yet do not enjoy that knowledge, it is a sin for which you will have to suffer. If a great soul, a Mahatma, calls you a fool, you have to suffer it. If the Mahatma calls anybody a fool, he has to suffer, and you are calling your Self something not knowledgeable yet, not knowing. That is the sin you commit. You are abusing your great soul.

I do not want to teach anything to anybody; I only hold up a mirror to those who come here. I will make you stand before the mirror and look at yourself. You have to get the vision of yourself in the light that is emanating from your own Self.

At bhajans we say, "You close your eyes and see that

everywhere He is standing, everywhere—inside, outside, up, down," and that you have to experience. If God is not residing in your body you will not be there.

Q: True. With this clear vision Maharaj can see and say. I can say, but not see.

M: If you do not recognize Him right now in this birth, several thousands of births will not give you the opportunity to know Him. At least now would you try to catch hold of Him with concentrated attention?

Q: One does try.

M: Who is that one and who is trying? Why are you worried about others? What about you, I am addressing this to you?

Q: That, to me, means the same thing as I answered. It's addressed to the Self and the Self is answering.

M: I have not asked you what the Self is doing. I am asking you what are you doing about you?

Q: Where is the difference? Are I and the Atma two different things?

M: You see, when you talk, you refer to the consciousness that is limited to your body. If you refer to the universal consciousness, that is Atma or God. Therefore you make it clear whether you refer to yourself as limited or unlimited.

Q: I am limited. As I have been told, I understand that I should say that I am unlimited. With the knowledge I have, with what teachers have told me, I am unlimited; and yet I know that I am limited.

M: Because you identify with the body, that is why you are conditioning yourself.

Q: True. I understand that. I know that I should get over that.

M: By your identification with the manifest body you have lost sight of your real nature. You must always be conscious of That. That state of consciousness is a natural thing, only don't break away from it.

You see, I don't disclose the acrobatics of the Vedas to the masses here. It's for other people to do, who dabble in body-mind.

Q: There is so much knowledge printed and disseminated here, there, everywhere; yet I would say that the majority of people live in darkness, in spite of that knowledge.

M: I don't ask anybody to follow any particular path. I just tell them to be what they are, in their natural, spontaneous state. Stabilize there, in the beingness.

Q: Those are exactly the same words as Baba uses. Just be.

M: Having served him for twenty-five years, why did you deny?

Q: I don't know.

August 25, 1979

Questioner: I am very confused, but I think it is best for me first to meditate.

Maharaj: It will be of no use; as long as there are questions it is better to bring them out. Suppression leads nowhere.

Q: Is there the need for the mind to become quiet?

M: You are before the mind is. Don't pay attention to the thoughts, pay attention to the consciousness. Thoughts will always flow because of the vital breath. Whatever thoughts are useful to you, you can make use of.

Q: Is it possible to attain a state where the mind is still?

M: Yes, that state you experience in deep sleep also. Through meditation you will attain it.

Q: There is no process involved?

M: With greatest interest you get absorbed in your Self. By giving attention only to your "I" consciousness you can reach it. Without giving attention to the body, but to the sense "I am."

Q: Is there a way as such? Each individual has his own path, doesn't he?

M: Your urge is to know your Self; I tell you the direct way.

Q: Which is that?

M: I just show you what you are prior to words. None of your experiences are eternal, so they cannot be the truth.

Q: Still humanity glimpses the Divinity.

M: This humanity is the untruth.

Q: But you can't deny the humanity, can you?

M: This human body is not the quality of the Self.

Q: It is its reflection.

M: In utter loneliness the touch of "I Amness" appeared. Just as in a small seed the entire tree is contained, the "I Amness" contains the whole creation.

Q: Is Maharaj able to see our level of awareness?

M: No, because I do not see you as an identity.

Q: But the level of awareness is a reality, not just a concept.

M: Do you say that by your own experience? These are ideas only. How can you say that the fire in the incense stick makes progress? It is there or it is not.

Q: There are the different distances until it is extinguished.

M: Ultimately, when it is extinguished, is there any progress after? Gone is gone.

Like the worms in the cow dung, the moment the cow dung dries they are finished, however much progress they have made.

Q: But the Maharaj is not a worm.

M: It is no different; this consciousness is a product of the food material. Whatever form the food material takes—man, monkey, or worm—doesn't matter; this consciousness is a product of the food material.

Q: What is the exact difference between the jiva, Brahma, and the Absolute?

M: You remove all the names and understand. These are all concepts, a chaotic confusion of words, nothing else. Whatever I tell you, this knowledge is never-ending, it has no beginning and therefore no end. All this is the product of the five elements, and the elements, including space, are substances. Space is like darkness, nothingness, like night. Out of it vital breath arose as a vibration.

This body has appeared on me automatically, without my willing it, and therefore I became puzzled. What I have experienced is—I am not that matter. That quality of being-ness, knowingness, which is a product of matter, gets extinguished and again goes into the atmosphere with increasing progression and the cycle continues. That beingness has gone to that state of matter, but it will not stay in that matter, it will take care that it goes back to its state of absolute subtlety.

August 27, 1979

Maharaj: Truth is timeless and beyond description. Whoever lives in that, and whatever he does, can the ego challenge the Truth that exists forever? The Truth cannot be challenged by anyone.

Sometimes a great wave sweeps over me, and I feel that I should make everything pure. But when I try to attend to it, I know that nothing can be done to change the fundamental Truth.

I see that consciousness comes into being, and that consciousness becomes the ether, as well as the food itself, and both perish into nothingness; so how is it going to be changed?

What is happening here is—out of the foliage, the grass, and the vegetation, the essence is eaten and another consciousness appears through that. Consciousness is the essence of the food that has been digested, and along with the food, that consciousness will also disappear.

During this limited span of life many have studied scriptures, performed austerities, and meditated. Whatever came out of that as thought has filled thousands of books. But once the attention is fixed on the substratum of consciousness, there is nothing left.

The consciousness that has come out of the five elements, through the body, is the quality of beingness, the knowledge that "I Am." That state of beingness will perish.

I have realized that I am living even when many cosmoses have come into existence and have been dissolved. All this I see, I know, and I understand. Yes, I know that I was always, ever, and abiding. Whatever has happened, I am here, ever-present.

Questioner: I am very anxious about my life, not satisfied.

M: You are immortal, you are not going to die; but give up the present meaning which you attach to life. You have only one thing to do: care for others as much as you care for yourself. Behave as if they were all yours; that is all you can do. There is no necessity for following any particular path, everything is the same. Think of that which is the center of the cosmos; don't let your attention stray in any way from this knowledge of beingness, "I Am."

Saints and Sages have assumed many prior lives, but those lives were limited, only for that particular period. All these beingnesses have appeared on ignorance and the whole consciousness is enjoying consciousness through ignorance, which has come out of ignorance. If you leave off the pride and the ego of that knowledge which you have got through ignorance, then everything is clear.

You have some experiences and you try to benefit from them, but remember that whatever is going to be of use to you ultimately is going to harm you. Wherever there is use, there is also dis-use in this world of duality.

Whatever you like is going to create harm for you. Whatever you like most is, in the end, going to be most harmful for you, even when it is Paramatman. Whatever appears on you as knowledge, and you try to understand it **and you like it, is going to be a cause of very great sorrow for you.**

When you come to the state of Parabrahman there are no desires, no likes or dislikes. That is Niskama Parabrahman.

Q: What is Niskama Parabrahman?

M: Because that Niskama [desireless] Parabrahman is, this manifestation has appeared and is doing what it pleases. Manifestation is Sakama [with desire], but the support of it is Niskama.

Q: If you want to reach that state, does it mean you also act like that—I don't care what happens, let it happen?

M: If you want to discuss it through the medium of the mind you are welcome to think of any meaning whatsoever. But whatever is done has limits. It is all limited activity.

If you want this experience you must insist on your Self, your own Atma-prema [Self-love]. Don't leave it for a moment. You insist. Do not pray to Gods or Goddesses, only see One. Keep on knowing that "I Am" and through that insistence you will know the state that you want to reach.

August 28, 1979

Questioner: I have heard many of these talks about the food that has become me, but the point is not very clear. What does it mean?

Maharaj: Every organic being, whether an insect or a human, depends on food. All these flowers, this foliage, is our antecedent state. We were in this state before, and gradually, out of the essences of all the bodies that we have taken in order to enjoy this beingness, our human body has been evolved. The "I Amness" is only the quality of that food body which you call "I." It has nothing to do with any other thing. It is the pure and simple quality of this beingness.

Q: Is it possible for this being which has come out of the food to do something original, something totally different?

M: Ramakrishna Paramahamsa performed austerities and became himself Jagadamba [Mother of the whole world]; others also have performed austerities and they understood the Truth. When they realized the Truth what could they do? So many great men have come, and what change, what different thing could they do? Whatever has happened, has happened when you were not knowing. The knowledge has come out of ignorance, or complete absence of knowledge, and no different course can be given to what is going on from infinity.

Q: My mind, intellect, and understanding are being modified, and I was thinking that Maharaj is giving me something totally new. Is he or not?

M: Whatever the changes or modification going on in your mind, or intellect, I am doing nothing that is different. I am only bringing before you newly what is infinitely ancient. There is nothing new.

During the process of questions and answers, even if you get angry with me, I will have absolutely nothing to say to you. When a mother takes her child of three months on her lap it kicks, it may slap her, it dirties her clothing. She merely takes the child in her arms and fondles it, and she even cleans herself only after cleaning the child. I look upon you exactly like that, even if your body is seventy-five years old.

Q: I see that point very clearly, and another simile comes to mind; that I am like an artist. Every time I paint something Maharaj says, "I see the connection," and in the process I get angry and maybe I throw paint on him. But he doesn't care, he is still smiling.

M: When the vital breath and body combination are present, this beingness is there. The beingness does not die. Take the harmonium player: because of the air in the harmonium sound is created; when the player removes his hand the air is gone and therefore no sound is there. Is the sound dead? It just disappears.

Q: Tell me exactly what is the connection between this quality of beingness and me.

M: The very essence of beingness is that knowledge "I Am," and still you say, "What is the connection?" The knowledge "I Am" is itself the quality of this body or the essence of food.

I will not teach whoever comes to me as if he were a mortal. I look upon him as immortal. There are lots of primary teachers in the world who can teach the alphabet. Even if I give him a slight injection or bite so as to find out who he is, the principle behind the knowledge "I Am" will be sufficient for him.

Q: People say that we should act with detachment. What is detachment?

M: If you want to know detachment you must realize the personality or individuality as melting away.

Q: The personality is so much with me, how am I to melt it away?

M: Find out the meaning of the Self. Try to understand the meaning of the Self by any means. Before this knowledge "I Am" appeared on you you were absolutely unattached. As soon as this knowledge dawned on you, you became attached to everything around you. Only that false "I" is attached. Everything is just happening, and that false "I" is taking the credit for doing things. You are the knower, not the doer. I will give you one piece of advice: do not do anything that will hurt another, that is all. You may not do anything to oblige them, or do good to them, but take care that you do not hurt anyone else. And that also is in this field of consciousness. Beyond that there is nothing.

If you become expansive with knowledge of the whole world and live for a thousand years to enjoy that knowledge, just remember that at the end of the thousand years all that knowledge is going to be extinguished. Even if this atom continues for a thousand years you must investigate as to when the point of the pen touched down to open this account.

Q: What opens the account?

M: It is ignorance which opens it. Ganapati [consciousness] is the entity which has started this account of hundreds of births. All these accounts will not tell you about Ganapati. You must find out the source of the consciousness.

The Maya is before the one. This account is made by one who has started counting with one. For counting somebody must be there to count, so he must be in existence before there was any number; Mula-Maya, Ganapati, investigate these. Ganapati is Lord of the primordial sound; sound and word are identical. One who understands the Ganapati is Brahman.

Today's subject is both difficult and very easy. You can learn anything outside yourself, but it is rather difficult to catch your Self. Once you catch it, once you know your own beingness, you will not forget it.

While you live, live fearlessly, because nobody has created you. Out of your own light you are living. Particularly, live with confidence in the Self.

August 31, 1979

Maharaj: What country are you from and who directed you here?

Questioner: I am from America. I have been visiting some Ashrams and some people I met told me about Maharaj and so I came. I have been studying the different philosophies for years.

M: Learning all these different philosophies has no meaning whatsoever. Unless you have a mirror in which you can see yourself, what is the good of it?

Q: A mirror is what I am looking for.

M: Those mirrors that you have had so far are all useless.

Q: No, they are not useless. They are just parts of the mirror that I can combine into one real big mirror.

M: Are you capable of carrying all that?

Q: No, not really.

M: You have the constant irritation in you that "you are." That itching is causing all the trouble, because you don't know exactly what you are. That is why you are roaming from place to place, in search of nobody. You must first find out when that itching started. Just sit here and listen awhile and then ask questions.

Q: Maharaj has said that everything is out of the food, and also that I am the creator of everything. Now I do not know whether I am the creator of everything or am something which has come out of the food.

M: Without asking anyone, whatever knowledge you have gained about yourself is absolutely correct.

Q: I experience difficulties.

M: It is beyond all difficulties. He who knows the difficulties is beyond them.

Q: A sense of great happiness arises in me when I hear the words of Maharaj.

M: This momentary happiness is of no use to you at all.

Q: Maybe I have not found it, but I am happy to hear about it.

M: All these ideas of yours are binding you. Once you understand that there is no knowledge, that it is all ignorance, you are on your proper level.

You have the idea that I have the knowledge; this is only an idea. Honestly speaking, there is no knowledge whatsoever. It is beyond all imagination, It has no attributes. It cannot be imagined at all.

Without the knowledge I am really very happy. By entertaining the idea "I have all the knowledge," it increases day by day, but that knowledge has no peace, no pleasure whatsoever. With several attributes that knowledge is violently spinning about, but I am not that knowledge. Every human being is told that it is his bounden duty to gain knowledge, but he will come to understand that this knowledge is of no use at all to gain his ultimate goal.

Q: What is God?

M: Everything you see is all Iswara [God].

Q: Around me I see the world.

M: Everything is Iswara, even the smallest atom is Iswara. In a large city like Bombay the gutters are full of dirt and litter that create a smell around you for some time; then it is gone, into the sky. The sky is ever there, it has no smell at all, it is pure and clean. The human body is dirt only. In course of time this body will go, that dirt will smell no more, it will be all pure sky, nothing will remain. But you are binding yourself, day by day, by your conceptual ideas: "I was born," "I will have rebirth," etc.; and you remain in all the misery.

Q: How can I get out of it?

M: How are you going to get out of it unless you know what you are?

Q: We see that the sky and the sun take care of the earth's dirt. Who is to say what will take care of my dirt?

M: You won't take delivery of any knowledge whatsoever. The storehouse is full of those concepts and ideas. All of them are dirt, and that is how you are binding yourself to the wheel of birth and death.

Q: Not all the concepts are dirty; some are very beautiful.

M: Remember that they have taken rise in you, who are ultimately the product of dirt.

Making a bundle of your concepts, you are busy in the world. You are not that "I" which is going about in a determined fashion that "I am so and so." You are behaving on the basis of that "I" which was absent before the birth, and will be absent after the death, of the body. That "I," limited by time, you have taken for granted. Go beyond the concepts and become idea-less.

September 1, 1979

Questioner: It seems to me that Maharaj is perpetuating the concepts by his way of giving us explanations.

Maharaj: All this conceptual cycle is created by you, because you have the concept "I Am," which you must eradicate yourself.

Q: Why create all this separation? Separating whatever there is from someone who is supposed to be different from it? This creates more concepts.

M: It is only saying that I am not this. When you are in deep sleep is there any experience of pleasure and pain or birth and death? What does that mean? It means that the concept "I Am" has vanished.

Q: I was wondering whether the relationship with Maharaj is breeding dependence? What we call laziness?

M: This knowledge is full of life; how can anyone be lazy? You can call the body or mind lazy, but how are you connected with them? In what way do you feel dependence on Maharaj?

Q: It is as if I am waiting for something to happen.

M: Find out the identity of that one who is waiting for something to happen.

Suppose there is a public well—that water [consciousness] is used by all. You have taken a portion of that water for your personal use. That consciousness which you have taken for yourself is the omniscient, the omnipotent, the omnipresent; and you must understand that. You cannot afford to be lazy.

When you have come thousands of miles from your country and have listened to this great knowledge, are you going to die as an individual of a particular country, caste, and color?

Understand that what is going around as your body and name is of the nature of the all-pervading consciousness. When you travel in a car are you the car?

Q: I understand.

M: You are the symbol of that consciousness; you need not understand it; it is conscious of itself. But you are limiting yourself to the body, that is all.

Q: If it is consciousness which is doing that, if consciousness itself is taking that limitation, there is nothing I can do about it.

M: That consciousness, through ignorance, has taken upon itself that limitation. That ignorance has to be discarded.

Q: The fact that you tell me that does not make me discover it. I have to discover it myself; otherwise I can talk to Sages for thousands of years without a single thing being changed. How do I discover it for myself?

M: It happens. If it is in your destiny, you will come here and listen to it, and the result will follow. Yesterday two people came here with this lady and then went away. It was not in their destiny. People come here with a predetermined concept of what they want. You come here as if to a tailor with an order for a suit of particular measurements, color, and material. But I will not give you what you want. I will not give you knowledge according to your predetermined requirements. I will only tell you to see yourself as you are, find out who you are.

Thousands of people come here; they will utilize this knowledge as it suits them only. This is not *the* Truth; it is the Truth as seen through their own concepts, according to their own point of view. This knowledge, filtered through their own point of view, is not knowledge, it is only a point of view.

Q: I give all my energy trying to understand what Maharaj says. I've been working very hard. Today I am at the point to stop. Essentially nothing has changed. I came with the idea that Maharaj is my Guru. Guru means the one who removes darkness, but darkness is still present. Now I feel that all my work has taken me nowhere. I feel that I have to start anew, from right now. How can I do it?

M: A man who was sitting in dense darkness wanted to remove the darkness and started praying to God. Then someone came and said: "What! Are you going to remove this darkness with your devotion? No. You have to bring the light." The light was brought and the darkness went away. Doing discipline is not necessary, but you must know that this is the Truth. "I Am the Truth," and that Truth has no beard or mustache; however it is the Truth, which you must realize. Truth has no form. If Truth had a form you would have gone and got it. Without effort, whatever is natural is that Truth.

Q: Is it that the Guru is only pointing the way?

M: You have to hold on to it, and gradually, when it grows, the light will envelop everything. The evidence of the Eternal is this transiency, the evidence of Truth is this untruth, and the evidence of Brahman is Maya.

Q: We ask questions and try to understand with the mind. How are we to go beyond this?

M: You are not the mind, nor the body. Who has this difficulty? Who has to go beyond? You were there before you asked this question. Before the appearance of the waking and sleep states, you are.

Q: How can I realize this?

M: As far as possible remember what you have heard today. Believe in it. It may not suit your requirements, but it is as it is. You have only to see it as it is and be blissful with it.

When you become that knowledge there will be nothing that you need anymore. You will be infinite yourself. I do not quote scriptures or give you the judgment of others, but whatever is, I tell you. You will never get evidence of Brahman's existence anywhere except within you.

What is evident one is likely to overlook. What I am saying is very clear and simple. You do not understand because you want something complicated.

Q: What exactly does Maharaj want to tell me?

M: You are the proof that there is God. If you are not there, there is no God. This "I Amness" is the proof. You think that it is limited to the body, but it is universal. It is the source of manifestation. You are the knower of the body. When this past disposition stops it is void and that void is witnessed by someone who is not void. One who knows that there is darkness—can he be darkness? If you keep absolutely quiet, then the concepts will be strangled to death.

I am doing nothing every day but telling you, in different

words each day, but always the same thing. It is for you to see. It is for you to understand. The flow is continually coming, but you are not hearing. In this very body, in this very birth, you must realize what I have told you. Leave all other concepts and hold on to this. When a sadhaka [spiritual aspirant] has become a Jnani it means that he has understood, finally and absolutely, what he is.

September 3, 1979

Maharaj: When death approaches you, remember that you have no shape and no color. "I am Nirguna [without attributes]"; this is the last thought that you should have. You know the body, but you are not the body. When you go to sleep, sleep with the remembrance of that truth. "Many impure thoughts have come and gone away, but I am immutable, I am infinite, I am the Truth." Sleep with these thoughts and all those impure thoughts are absolved.

Don't go off to sleep as a slave to the mind; be its master. Form this habit, become absolutely detached and master of your mind.

Questioner: How do I eradicate fear?

M: The fear named birth has to be eradicated. You come here with acquisitions of various kinds of education. I want to defeat that acquisition of yours and that food which you have taken. Before that food and that knowledge, what were you? I want you to think about this.

Q: What is consciousness?

M: The activity of your beingness, and the activity that you see, of the whole world. This consciousness is without any color, but where there is a personality, it takes the color of that particular personality. When the beingness goes, that colorful personality merges into that colorless one, consciousness. There is no difference in the consciousness, it is all one, but we call it by different names.

It is all knowledge, all consciousness, it has no measurements. When the taste of that beingness which you are feeling today merges into that universal consciousness it does not have the consciousness of limited individuality. It has not come from anywhere and it does not go anywhere.

You are existence which is without any desire or objective; that Great One where several manifested universes have come and gone.

Q: I have been reading and studying *I Am That*.[1] I still feel dissatisfied with my way of living.

M: Have you tried to find out the reason?

Q: No, I guess that I love my personality too much.

M: You still feel that you are the body-mind; that is why you are feeling unhappy.

Q: That's right.

M: You have been reading with the mind. Now, whenever you read the book consider that you are the universal consciousness, and from that point of view do your reading and studying. Read it from the point of view that you have no form or color, that you are the light.

Q: I cannot read anymore if I think that I am not the body and mind.

M: Don't be anxious as to whether you will be able to read or not. You just do what I have told you and gradually things will unfold. Some people are quite ready to take it, and some people have to be beaten and still they don't understand, but if you are ready, it will unfold. Some people are so tough they are like the Indian dish poppadum; it has to be beaten a lot, and even then the dough is so tough that it has to be rolled very forcefully, and then it is fried. Some people have to be taught in this laborious way, while others are quite ready and will accept immediately they are told. Others just listen and concentrate on my words, and suddenly there is an explosion.

[1] Chetana Pvt., Ltd., Bombay.

You must meditate on that "I Am" without holding on to the body and mind. As you nursed at your mother's breast when you were a baby, so you nurse at this "I Am," the knowledge of your beingness.

Q: For four years I have been trying to remember to stay in the "I Am."

M: Will you do what I have told you today?

Q: Read the book?

M: Whatever you have heard. Will you live like that, without the sense of being a body-mind?

Q: I'm ashamed that I was very afraid to come here, because you never know what is going to happen. Maybe nothing, maybe many things. So, I am a little nervous.

M: Your fear will be completely destroyed. Not only will you not be nervous, but your fear itself will go. You must nurse at the knowledge "I Am." Remember and meditate on this also: "I have no fear, I am beyond fear."

Q: I have fear for all the people. If I am walking through a city in Holland, for example, I am afraid for all the people.

M: I am telling you that this fear will gradually lessen, and will go completely, because I say so. The medicine for that fear is my word.

Q: What is bondage?

M: Mind is the very foundation of your bondage and liberation. The Muslims have the concept that after death the soul is confined to the tomb until the dissolution of the world; therefore they provide for that soul. In the Christian religion also they say that man, once buried in the grave, will be awakened only on doomsday and judgment will be given.

Q: Does that really happen to those people?

M: If they die with that concept it must happen, because the mind creates everything. The mind creates bondage and it also liberates. Today suppose I am not able to think, my mind is not very clear. What does it mean? My food essence is rather dull today. It is not getting into combustion in proper order; therefore the thinking faculty is also dull. This mind faculty also pertains to the body essences and I am not that.

Understand clearly "You are" and "I am"; these feelings are the products of this gross earth. Out of the earth comes vegetation and the essence of "I Amness." That "I Amness" disappears when the body drops off, because essentially it is only a product of the food essence.

September 6, 1979

Maharaj: You come here with your concept "I am like this," so I have to start demolishing it, to throw it overboard.

The Absolute does not know itself, but the Absolute is offered an opportunity to understand itself through this food product, the "I Am."

Questioner: Before I came here I expected to be full of love, but I feel weak and tired.

M: This is because of the demolition process. To start with, you must be completely dismantled and rebuilt. Before the seed is planted the ground must be cultivated and fertilized. Only after plowing the ground and planting the seed will the sprouting take place. The demolishing process is necessary; what remains is only consciousness, and then the sprouting takes place.

Whenever foreigners come here they raise the question of love. "I Amness" is love only. You have assumed this shape, this flower of "I Amness," out of love only. The very core of all atoms is permeated by that knowledge "I am." Embrace all the atoms of the universe with the feeling that all of them have come inside us in the form of the knowledge "I Am."

You are listening to this knowledge of something which cannot be experienced by the body-mind consciousness in words through your body-mind consciousness.

Whenever you speak, you first identify yourself with

something, but that "I" is not going to last, it is not honest, it will not be eternal.

Whatever I am telling you will be absorbed only by those who have the ground already prepared for it. Even those who think they have understood have not understood as I mean for them to understand.

Q: Yesterday I couldn't sleep. When I was lying on my bed I kept hearing sounds and seeing lights. I was scared, sweating. I thought I was dying.

M: Whatever is happening is happening as it should. Even if whatever you felt was dying actually was dying, you were not dead. Keep that firmly in mind.

What sort of love is advocated in your religion?

Q: Love thy neighbor.

M: Your religion advocates that you love every being out of the love for God. Christ said to love your neighbor as yourself. How do you put that into practice?

Q: By sometimes coming here. That love is here.

M: The love is in the most purified form when there is no difference between the lover and the beloved. In all this world of yours what is the cause of the most suffering?

Q: Duality.

M: When did this duality start?

Q: With the first perception of something other than myself.

M: The beginning of duality is when you know you are. This is the primary duality, the very source of illusion.

Don't just listen to me meekly. Ask questions. What knowledge would you like to acquire?

Q: Of sin and merit.

M: That by which you feel happy and satisfied is merit, and that by which you are disturbed or dissatisfied is sin.

Q: If a man commits a sin and does not feel sorry for it, is it still a sin?

M: Don't talk from the standpoint of a person, a human being, an illusion! When did you get to know about merit and sin? Only after you were given a concept.

Q: If you do something wrong, do you suffer immediately or in your next life?

M: You may have to suffer immediately, and definitely in your next birth. The beginning of suffering was with the memory that you are.

Q: Those who commit sins do not appear to be suffering.

M: This is your concept, but inside there are traumatic experiences.

Q: How do we face our problems in daily life?

M: According to your own identity with that Self, carry out your duties. Look upon all as your Self.

Q: In the life of a lawyer so many things happen every day. There is always trouble.

M: You are speaking from the body-mind sense. Get out of that.

Q: And then do whatever I like?

M: Then you will behave according to your own worthiness.

Q: So once you clearly understand the knowledge of the Self, the difficulties disappear. Then everything goes on automatically.

M: True. Then why do you ask questions?

Q: Are there no activities in that state?

M: Then you will know that not a leaf moves without you. Because of you all activities take place.

Q: There is talk of equanimity and tranquility, but it seems to me that with suffering there is more of an urge to realize. Kunti, the mother of Pandavas, asked Krishna for suffering so that she could remember him. Can I have your comments?

M: How long have you been here? That is meant for the ignorant. If you find your own identity such questions will not arise. Such ideas are given to instill courage into the ignorant. Not for you. The next question would be: "Who was the priest who performed the marriage of Rama and Sita?"

Q: If Self-knowledge is the proper approach, where is the place for devotion?

M: They are not different—Bhakti and Jnana. This is realized only when you realize your own Self. Because "I Amness" is there you have devotion to God. The process of loving the Self by the Self is taken up by devotion to Rama, Krishna, Christ, etc., and its fruition is when the Self realizes the Self. Then you know that everything is the Self only.

Q: Is it any help to pray that the soul rest in peace?

M: It is only a concept. For a dead person is there a soul left so that he is going into peace? Out of love for the dead person you take a bowl of milk and offer it to the dead soul. Is he going to come and drink it? It is only to give you satisfaction. Why inquire about what occurs after death? What are you today? This illusion always keeps you away from your own Self. You are always inquiring about everything outside, but you do not try to find out what you are. All during your life you have held different identities for yourself. After your birth you perceived that you were a child, then a teenager, an adult, middle-aged, and old. None of these identities has remained with you. Whatever you hold onto as "myself" will disappear.

This is to be understood. A Sat-Guru must guide you. He only is the Sat-Guru who has fully understood.

You have to understand the contradiction clearly. Whatever I am expounding, I am driving at something.

If you say that you have understood it has not clicked. You must come to a state of "I have not understood anything." You must go beyond this understanding stage, come to a stage beyond. You must come to this conclusion: the various stages from childhood up to old age—whatever you have understood and got stabilized in as your identity—has proved false. Likewise, whatever you have tried to understand during your spiritual search will prove false. Therefore nothing is to be understood. Deliberate on this.

September 7, 1979

Questioner: What are we to do today?

Maharaj: Witness that consciousness, that mischievous, illusive consciousness because of which you observe various

stages. It's very simple. This consciousness was not there earlier and it is going to disappear. Still you will be there and
witness that consciousness. You, the Absolute, are the perfect state. You are not the consciousness, nor are you in the
consciousness, which is full of wants and needs.

Another way of understanding: Whatever knowledge I
have acquired through bhajans, devotion, etc., is surrendered
to the knowledge of God, but I am not that. I don't come
within the perfume of that knowledge or consciousness. All
is surrendered to the consciousness itself and I am apart
from it. "I surrender all my knowledge, including myself and
consciousness, to that manifest consciousness Brahma." Creation itself is Brahma, the sacrificial fire is also Brahma and
the sacrificer is Brahma.

Q: The only thing I understand is that we are the Reality, not the body-mind. I am always thinking of that.

M: Tell me about your knowledge of this.

Q: It is very difficult. That is all there is and we are
always that.

M: You find it very difficult to describe because you cannot give it a name or form. What is it of which you cannot
give a description?

Q: I just feel the presence of that "I Amness," that existence; I cannot describe it.

M: You cannot see that knowingness, but that sees everything else. That consciousness is the same in everything and
everywhere. Having once realized this with conviction, can
you make use of it?

Q: No, no use can be made of it.

M: Whatever happens in the world—will it have the
same attraction for you?

Q: No. I used to be concerned with whatever was happening, but it does not concern me now.

M: Things are happening in the world just as they used
to happen, but one has realized that one has no name or
form and therefore no activities. Whatever is happening in
the world is in the nature of a dream. The individual personality is lost. One who knows this cannot be interested in

improving such a world. He does not concern himself with the behavior in the world.

A person may have the brightest intellect in the world and, with the aid of that intellect, collect the maximum information about the world, but all that will be useless because the basis is false. After listening to the significance of these words, have you reached your original state? *You.*

Q: No.

M: That is because of your identify with, and pride in, your body-mind.

Q: Why do we see a world? Why do we see wrongly?

M: When you ask this question, are you not aware of yourself, don't you have an identify with your body?

Q: Yes, I have.

M: Give up this idea.

Q: How can I?

M: There is really nothing to give up. You have a name; you think you are that name but you are not.

Q: What is the function of the name? my body? my personality?

M: You don't have a personality. It's all in the mind.

Q: I do have a mind and my mind tells me that I have a personality. What can I do?

M: It's not the mind, it's the vital breath that makes you feel you are a separate entity. Vital force gives rise to the thoughts, otherwise there is no mind. The breath gives rise to the thoughts in the world and you are only watching it.

So long as you identify with the body-mind this subject is far beyond your understanding. You must go beyond the mind.

Q: I don't want to go beyond.

M: Come here only if you are prepared to listen without the body-mind identity, otherwise you are wasting your time. Don't come here unless you are prepared to give up this identity.

Q: But I keep on finding myself here!

M: All right, do come here, but keep on pondering about this: that you are not the body.

Q: I think about it all the time, but my thinking does not take me further.

M: Keep thinking and discriminating. When the body dies, you do not die.

Q: It must be a part of myself which I have never known. I just know my body, my name, my personality. That's all I know.

M: You keep thinking about it and listening. Read about it, study about it.

September 8, 1979

Questioner: I don't know what I am, I only know I am in pain—that much I know.

Maharaj: These are the opposites of pain and pleasure.

Q: This is slightly different from ordinary pain.

M: Some liking of yours has been contaminated; therefore you experience that feeling.

Q: How did Maharaj know this?

M: That cannot be explained. I cannot say how I woke up or went to sleep.

Q: Can you help me in my pain?

M: Forget the body consciousness. You need not be after pleasure. Whatever you call the pleasure is not the Ultimate.

Q: I am not after pleasure, or happiness, but this thing which is troubling me should go.

M: It is not there. It is only your imagination, your concept that you have that pain. There is nothing purer than you are. That pain is only your imagination, an illusion, a concept.

Q: How to throw away that concept?

M: What is there to throw away? That you were born— how did you get that concept?

Q: I should ignore it?

M: Only know, only observe, be the witness—nothing else is to be done. Don't attempt anything. Only know what you are.

Q: So I have no salvation, I must witness all this trouble?

M: Yes. You are to look straight at the face of it, the origin of it, the whole of it, and find out from where it is. Look at that center from where this knowledge has appeared on you. Concentrate on that only.

When you reach that core you will find rays of light emanating from it. Whatever you see is only the play of light. Merge into that center, be one with it.

Q: What will happen to the universe all around me that I have rejected?

M: You are the center, and when you turn inside you will find that all the universe you see is only through that.

Q: I see that Maharaj has regulated his own life. Why does he not tell us what we should do from morning to night?

M: Give no attention to what you should do from morning to night. Just pay no attention to this; you are not the body-mind.

Q: Then how is it that Maharaj has regulated his life?

M: I am beyond time and life. The life of the universe depends on me; I don't depend on the universe.

Q: Maybe so, but what we see is a well-regulated life.

M: I am untouched by the five elements. Apparently it seems that I might be rolling in actions, but there is no action for me.

Once you get a glimpse of your true state you must stabilize there for eternity. My mother told me that I am a boy; she never asked me to memorize it, to repeat "I am a boy." She told me only once, and I remembered it. You need not repeat, "I am not the body." Once you understand it, it is finished. You must be as firmly convinced that you are not the body as you are sure that you are not going to deliver a baby because you are a male. You will never entertain the idea at any time that you are going to deliver a child.

Q: What should I meditate on?

M: Meditate on the fact that you are, on your beingness.

Q: Why do you call this "I Amness" the food essence?

M: This "I Amness" is only a signboard indicative of the Absolute, but the signboard is not you.

The body is a doll made out of the raw material of this manifest universe. It is continuously changing and evaporating into the manifest universe. When this gets exhausted, it only transforms itself into space. When this body is completely transformed into space there is no intellect. That intelligence is there only with the body. Out of the space it gets formed again. In the process of that formation there is no intelligence.

Q: Is there no such thing as time?

M: Your "I Amness" defines the time. It is only an idea.

M (to another): Have you brought any questions?

Q: Last year I came to India to find a Guru who could lead me to Self-Realization. I came with the idea of finding a form who would give me detailed instructions, step by step. When I met Maharaj, instead of finding a Guri with a form, all I walked away with was an empty frame or a mirror. I found I didn't have any form, anything. Just pure space that changes all the time. When I think of Maharaj, sometimes I see him as myself, sometimes I see him as nothing. The person that I see in front of me changes all the time. There is nothing I can point at and say, "That is he." It is frightening, and the fear has been growing.

M: What you have said is quite appropriate, quite correct. Whatever you observe is nothing else but your Self only. Get rid of the body image as yourself. Whatever you have seen is your Self.

Q: Often the concepts, the ideas that are in the books, or that are discussed here, come to my mind, or his image comes to my mind. Immediately after, not before, the feeling comes that there is nothing there, that what I'm hearing is not what it is, but it's only after thinking of him that I feel this space.

M: Who realizes that nothing is, that everything is gone? And when everything is gone, what remains?

Q: That's what is frightening.

M: When everything goes, you are the Real.

Q: As a concept I understand that. For a second I realize, and then I go back to the unreal. I attach myself to my family, my wife, my children. It's a habit, I go back.

M: You are so used to the support of concepts that when your concepts leave you, although it is your true state, you get frightened and try to cling to them again. That is the meeting point of that immanent principle and the Eternal, the borderland. Why is the intellect puzzled then? That beingness which you are experiencing is melting away. When that concept of "I Am" goes, intellect also goes. So the intellect gets that frightening experience of "I am going."

Q: How to overcome the fright?

M: Just watch that moment. One who feels "I am dying" is not a Jnani. Your true state is beyond the primary concept of "I Am." Consciousness is the primary concept, but this "I Amness" or consciousness is the product of the food body. You, the Absolute, are not that.

Death comes to the quality of "I Amness," which is a product of the food, but the Absolute prevails always. This is the Ultimate knowledge. This knowledge was expounded by Lord Krishna to Arjuna on the battlefield, the horses poised, on the point of battle. He never advocated to Arjuna that he should shave his head and go into the forest and perform tapas. Nothing of the sort. Once you understand this ultimate knowledge, then do what you like. Lord Krishna said, "With true dynamism you fight this battle"; and I say, once you understand this, you carry out your worldly life with full enthusiasm, full of zest, but understand that your true identity is beyond this quality of "I Amness."

For a Jnani the moment of so-called death is the most blissful, because he is going to the very source of bliss. Eternity is bliss, the very ocean of nectar, immortal.

September 9, 1979

Maharaj: After you became conscious of your body and your beingness you gathered impressions from your environment and observed the manifested world around you. After deliberating on the panorama of the world, of yourself in it, you must have come to some conclusion of your own.

All your behavior is dependent on your identification with the body, which depends on the knowledge "I Am." The "I Am" depends upon the food essence sustaining your body.

This is your capital for going about in the world. This consciousness of beingness which you are now experiencing is dependent on the essence of the food you eat. When you can no longer assimilate that food your vital breath becomes weaker and will one day go, along with the consciousness that "you are." You will solve this puzzle if you are eager to deliberate on it. There was absolutely no experience of yourself or the world before you experienced body or the food. This manifestation is beginningless. First was born the sky; out of the sky came the air; out of the air, the light and heat; out of that heat the water; and out of the water whatever was became the earth from which the whole of life sprouted. These five elements together are responsible for this great manifestation. Consciousness is the quality of the essence of the food that is in all the five elements together.

Questioner: Then the different qualities of the food should produce different qualities of that consciousness?

M: The five elements differ from each other. Guna is different in each form. When that consciousness is limited to the body it seems to be different, but when it knows itself it will merge into the universal consciousness, which is all-embracing.

Q: How is the illusion born?

M: How is the shade of a substance born? It comes out

of all the substances that make up the body. This Maya is nothing but love for that beingness.

Q: We are not able to step out of that trap.

M: You stick to what you are in the beginning, without embellishments or attachments. It is an imaginary trap that you are caught in.

Q: What do we do to get this experience?

M: Don't do anything. Just be in your "I Amness" and do not give it the shape of your body.

Q: Why should we hold on to the "I Amness"?

M: You must know the consciousness of your beingness. By doing that you will be like the man who has caught Brahma in the hand. As a fisherman catches the fish in his net, so you will be after knowing your beingness.

Q: The mind-ego always makes it difficult to know myself.

M: Mind does not exist without your consciousness. It is all a matter of words. Vital breath has given birth to mind.

Q: Why do we have to hold on to this "I Am" if we already know that we are beyond it? "I Am" is only a concept.

M: When did it occur to you that "I Am" is only a concept?

Q: I became aware that everything is concepts and that I don't have to live with concepts.

M: There is no question of being with this or that. Just be.

Q: We hear that we are to live as what we are already. While we are here, in this room, it is very easy to cast off what we are not, but how are we to live outside in a world that does not really exist?

M: You will come to realize that you do nothing. Everything happens; and you will come to know that you are only the observer of what happens. Just be. Where is the world for those who have realized? The world is in that beingness.

Q: I do not have to do anything?

M: What have you done so far?

Q: So far our relationship is of "have to" and "be." Is it to "be" first and then "have to"?

M: That will look after itself. I only show you the state of affairs; what you do after that is your own business. In one way you will understand that the whole supply of everything is through your Self and in another way, you will have lost everything.

September 10, 1979

Questioner: Why is Maharaj asking us to condemn the gross form?

Maharaj: I do not. Everything—the dirt, the body—is myself, but the process of transformation is continually going on. That gross form is again transformed into space; the cycle goes on.

Q: Why should we worry about accelerating the cycle?

M: Who is accelerating?

Q: We are all doing it.

M: Since your recognition of yourself is from your toes to the crest of your head, who has asked you to take the worry?

Q: There are two things: the world and my pain.

M: This is the seat of your body identification.

Q: I should ignore everything around me?

M: When you reach that particular level of understanding and assimilating, you will experience it and enjoy it. But once you transcend it, you will evacuate it like fecal matter. I have become Brahma-deva, having understood the quality of Brahma-deva, but if there is something better than the Brahma-deva quality I will attain it, rejecting this, etc. These are the landmarks or levels of different worthiness.

For me, there is no question of any movement. I am also dynamic and the nonexhaustible itself. Although the flow is there I cannot exhaust it. Everything in the world merges in me, settles down and takes rest.

No doubt Gurus are very important, very significant, but finally they merge into space. Whatever you embrace and cling to is going to go. Give up everything and understand what you are.

Q: I have a question. Yesterday Maharaj said that if a person wants to realize what he is, he should just embrace the "I" consciousness. Is that similar or equal to the relationship between a disciple and a Guru?

M: When you become one with that knowledge you will realize that the knowledge "I Am" is the very Guru of the universe.

Q: I ask because I feel love and respect for Maharaj, and I feel that he responds too, in a very simple, uncluttered manner. I have needed him to help me start embracing the "I" consciousness, I have needed his wisdom. My feeling for him has grown. I need to understand the relationship between the Guru and the disciple.

M: Whatever is to be known is contained in that very thing itself. What has been said is correct.

Q: Since I was here before, his image, everything he said, is coming all the time, but I also remember that he said that I must be free of concepts, even that of a Guru.

M: What you say is very good. The Guru is the manifestation of the knowledge which you will also be in course of time.

Q: I accept what you are saying. Should I act or just let things come and go?

M: There is nothing to be done. Let it flow, just watch, do nothing about it. The sun is shining, the rays go where they go. There is a doll made of sugar. That doll is sugar only. Similarly, when you see the image of a Guru, it represents knowledge only, your consciousness. The image may be of the Guru, Lord Krishna, Christ, etc.; it is the manifestation of the knowledge which you are.

Q: In this process, knowledge of all types, concepts of all types, cosmic as well as personal, come to my mind unbidden. When they flow they seem to touch people, relationships change. Things happen in the world and I don't know exactly how to cope with them.

M: Acting as a personality, an illusion, would not be correct. Whatever actions happen through you, without your involvement as a personality are the appropriate, spontaneous actions.

Q: In my traveling and searching in the past I have come across different kinds of Gurus. One who teaches Mantra Yoga, Kundalini Yoga, etc. What is the underlying reality? Must the seeker know about the Kundalini awakening or the chakras?

M: When you stabilize in the knowledge of your beingness, all other knowledge becomes available to you.

Q: Wherever I go this Kundalini knowledge seems to follow me. I want to know whether I should throw it out or look at it.

M: Throw it out, but hang onto your being, your own Self. Don't accept anything except your being. Just be. The only pure knowledge is of the Self.

Q: I found the Gayatri mantra in a book; I have a certain fondness for it, a certain use.

M: Don't make use of anything except the knowledge "I Am." Forget everything else. Consider a magnificent tree with many branches and leaves. Go to the root and not to the branches.

Q: Why have Gurus always had a certain kind of initiation with disciples?

M: That is their nature. After marriage the children multiply—that is the nature of wedded love. The Guru-disciple initiation is a natural process.

Q: Is there initiation here?

M: Oh yes. You are given a certain sentence and you are asked to be alert and to remain as the meaning of those sacred words.

Q: What must one be, or do, to reach that position?

M: Only have the firm conviction that the meaning of

the sacred sentence is your Self. You must be alert, your attention must be present.

Q: Is it wrong to ask to be initiated?

M: There is no question of wrong. If you want it, it will be granted. As a matter of fact, that is the formal initiation, but all this talk is a process of initiation only.

Q: I am aware of that, but I would like the formal initiation.

M: It will be granted. But with this you are given something more than formal initiation. The whole idea is that you must be like that. You must pay attention to the meaning of the word. That you are this only, nothing else.

September 11, 1979

Maharaj: Man takes upon himself all these concepts of sin and merit. He binds himself with all sorts of concepts. The consciousness takes an infinite manifestation of forms according to the concepts of the individual. What I am trying to do is to correct that concept idea.

Questioner: What is the cause of the next birth?

M: Once this beingness, the "I Know," has been extinguished and merged into the universal consciousness, what do you point to as the seed of the next birth?

Q: Isn't it desire which causes rebirth?

M: Haven't those desires and passions been assimilated into what is called the atmosphere, and has it not been universal in that sense? Where is the individuality? Where is the seed for rebirth? If you look at what matter is, it is solidified water, so when you talk of rebirth, what is it that is going to take rebirth? See this metal; is it water? You will not call it water, though it has come out of water ultimately. So if you want to find out about yourself, discriminate properly. Find out exactly what you are. Why worry about the next birth? Find out what you are now. Leave out all irrelevance.

All these creations are taking place out of that principle which is subtler than space. That ancient principle itself takes birth in various forms. These are the incarnations; there are no other reincarnations.

You come here wanting some kind of palatable knowledge. I am not going to deliver it; I am going to place factual knowledge before you. Right from childhood you have attained various stages and all of them are gone. Whatever you have attained will go, so what are you going to hold onto as yourself?

If you want to be what you are, it is free and plentiful and available without any difficulty; but if you want to be something other than what you are, it is difficult.

Q: But we read and hear of rebirth.

M: Have you experienced death and rebirth? Those are the ideas of others. Find out for yourself what you are; you should not accept the answers from other people. You can think for yourself. Ponder it, find out what you are.

Presently you are the manifest knowledge. When you try to imbibe that, that itself will give you all the knowledge, but you must dwell there only.

Q: What does "I Am" connote?

M: It means there are three states, waking, dream, and deep sleep. "I Am" means you are these three states; when these are gone the memory is also gone, so where is the question of reincarnation? When the body is dead it decomposes, many worms are formed. They are formed because the essence of the five elements is present and out of it life emerges. How is the life indicated? Everything, the whole cosmos, is full of this life force that is expressed through the food body. Therefore the "I Am," the life force of insects, animals, etc., is already present, only the expression is attained through this objective food body.

The appearance of this primary concept "I Am" is the beginning of duality. I started counting with myself, before this counting starts, That has no number, That is the Absolute. With that little movement "I Am" this counting started.

Q: I understand completely, intellectually, but how can I realize it?

M: Who understands the intelligence—and with what?

Q: Our need is to enter into that fully conscious state— we call it super-consciousness. Can we enter into that super-consciousness consciously? Or must the consciousness be tied down to enter it?

M: I drop into sleep spontaneously, I have not studied the art of sleeping. Similarly this consciousness subsides into no-consciousness.

Q: Are we to make efforts? Is this art of entering super-consciousness by Grace?

M: Did you put in any effort to get this body shape? It came automatically, spontaneously. This is also spontaneous, but you want to make effort, to employ some special skills to go into that Absolute state, to be.

Q: What is right meditation?

M: The right meditation is when you contemplate your Self. There should be no concepts or images while you are contemplating. Brahman is without concepts.

Q: I try to allow my mind to wander and slowly it comes to steadiness for a second. I can sometimes witness the thoughts, but I am not reaching the "I Am."

M: What you must witness is not your thoughts but the consciousness "I Am." Everything is an expression of the "I Am," but you are not that ; you are prior to the "I Am."

Q: "I Amness" means all this chaotic worldly state; so when am I in a position to just observe the "I Amness"?

M: Follow Arjuna. Could there be more chaotic conditions than on the battlefield? Right in the midst of the battlefield Arjuna attained ultimate understanding.

Q: We have to observe the chaotic condition without naming it chaotic, just bear with it quietly, within and without. Can we go beyond chaos and bring the new order within ourselves, without our knowledge?

M: Yes. When you are apart from consciousness it is

peace only. Whatever you try to design out of your own concept or intellect is useless. The Eternal has no fragrance of "I Am" about Itself. It does not know It is.

Q: I want a little help of the communion type to be spiritually influenced, just for expediting the process of concentration within me.

M: It is already happening, otherwise you would leave. Why are people coming here, spending a lot of money, traveling many miles? Why do they sit here? Is there any attraction of beauty here? People come here when the Absolute is opening up. It is opening up unknowingly—what happens knowingly will not last. It is unknowingly, spontaneously opening up and you will not understand that. Whatever you understand is not going to remain. As a child did you know that you were taking a shape or a design and that later you would undergo all these stages? Everything happens spontaneously.

Q: What does seeing purple light in meditation mean?

M: These are all images created out of your own illumination. That light might take the form of Lord Krishna, Christ, Rama, etc., but it is Self light, your creation.

Q: It has no particular purpose?

M: You are seeing your own light. All scriptures are sung in praise of that principle, but you, the Absolute, are not that principle. No doubt that is a very significant step; that principle is great, but I, the Absolute am not that.

September 14, 1979

Questioner: In the process of meditation when one reaches the silence and asks "Who am I?" there comes a profounder silence where the notion "I" does not arise. Is this the state, and if so, can one have flashes of it prior to Self realization?

Maharaj: These experiences are in the realm of your birth state.

Q: The state that I am referring to is the state where birth is forgotten, as are the name and form.

M: What you have described of samadhi, or meditation, is correct, but it is still the product of the body-mind imagination. Whatever experiences you have in meditation, of that silence also, is confined to the realm of consciousness. Consciousness is born and it will go. You are prior to it.

Q: It is also said that the Self is Self-effulgent, that it is light, and that the consciousness appears by a reflection of that light. If one were to pursue the light, could one find the state to which Maharaj is alluding?

M: Whatever is manifest before you has come out of that consciousness.

Q: I was talking about a Self-effulgent light which equates itself with the Self. If one is a seeker of Truth, by finding that light would one find the Truth?

M: There is the true Awareness, from which comes consciousness, which is your feeling "I Am"; be one with your consciousness and that is all that you can do, the Ultimate state must come to you. You can only watch whatever happens—there is nothing you can do to get it.

Q: Is there in Maharaj's awareness a Self-effulgent light that does not constrict his awareness but is part and parcel of it?

Translator: He has confirmed that earlier. Those are only names—you can call it true Awareness, the Ultimate state, or the effulgent light—the meaning is the same.

Q: It is not literal?

Translator: It is not literal.

Q: Many of the religious texts of Advaita Vedanta express the notion that as one becomes Self-aware there is a light which permeates, and that the light which the world, or Maya, has is a reflection of that primordial light. Is that not literal?

M: Maya is the expression of that One which cannot be described. Consciousness is manifesting itself through all this, and you are before the consciousness. The consciousness is the soul of this manifest world, and you, the Absolute, are the soul of the consciousness.

Whatever you may have read is only the concepts of the writers. Does it tally with your personal knowledge?

Q: No, these are the guidelines toward achieving the sense of the "I Am." They also say that all Gurus are one.

M: Guru is the same all-pervading consciousness "I Am." The Sat-Guru has gone beyond all these concepts, including the primary concept "I Am."

Q: Can this going beyond be done on a step-by-step basis, or does it happen immediately?

M: You say a child is born when the body arrives. Didn't it take nine months to develop that body? If you consider the nine months it is step-by-step, but the birth itself is sudden.

Q: All right, there is a gestation period; is that analogically correct with the facts?

M: I have an analogy that even the nine months is not correct. You Are before the gestation period. The whole thing is Maya: nobody is born and nobody dies—it is a distortion.

Q: That is true, but some of us are more distorted than others. The question is how to become less distorted.

M: Back again to the original position—nothing is to be done. Be in your beingness and everything that is to happen will happen. You must have a deep yearning to attain the Truth. You must have the intense need to understand. To such a person, the Guru arrives and breaks the shell.

Q: Yes, but there is another injunction that one should remain desireless; the yearning is also a desire.

M: At that moment it is a necessity. To become desireless is the last desire and it must exist.

Q: How should this yearning manifest itself?

M: Do you have to be told that you are awake?

Q: Sometimes, yes.

M: You know it.

Q: Well, sometimes the sadhaka has to be hit on the head.

M: I agree. Your beingness is something to which you are entitled. That is your primary capital in life and that will do whatever is to be done. That state which was yours before you were born, and which is yours after the body dies, is your permanent property. Your "I Amness" is consumed in that Ultimate capital of yours.

Q (Another questioner): I have a question. Why do I feel sad when I see that my parents and the Guru are only concepts? I have so much love, and to see them as concepts brings a feeling of pain.

M: There is no other concept except that "I am born"; at the root of all parents and Gurus is that primordial illusion.

Q: Things that are ugly go easily, but not so the things that one loves; that brings pain.

M: These are the pangs of things which should not have been done and are done, and which should have been done and were not done; hence these pains. That attachment should not be body-bound; overcome that sense of body identification. Love for the Guru is without the feeling of duality.

Q: There are so few Self-realized beings and so many sadhakas wishing to become realized. Why are there so few who have achieved success?

M: Everything is spontaneous, this manifestation has no cause; therefore nothing can be pointed out as a cause for your question as to why few become Siddhas. This question cannot be answered.

You try to be that love which is not conditioned by the body-mind. If you are that love, it is total, complete love, but if it arises out of your body-mind, that is the root cause of your misery. Detachment comes only after you are free from bodily love. Be free from the body-mind state and be in the state of love, and that will be the source of all bliss.

Q: Sometimes I believe there is a communion—the highest communion—with the Sat-Guru in the silence.

M: It's a good taste, but it is personal.

Q: Perhaps it might be personal until one becomes absorbed by what one adores; then it may become impersonal.

M: Did you see us worship this morning?

Q: Yes, I did.

M: There is no darkness, there is no daylight, there is no deep sleep, there is no waking state, no hunger, no thirst. That is the state, but all this is my expression. You feel that you are in that, but I feel that I am not in that. I worship, I do bhajans, but I am not in that. My true state is beyond that.

Q: I felt like the Self was worshiping the Self.

M: Whatever you call it is all right, but it is still a concept. Any concept you utter frames your future; therefore don't have any concepts. You are already the Ultimate, don't try to be something.

Q: What does one do about the practical side of this relative existence? That is, the working, the achieving, the goal-oriented society that we live in, the families that we have; what is to be done about them?

M: This world expression is out of the five-elemental consciousness, whose responsibility it is to take care of this manifest world. The world is the expression of your consciousness, but you are not the consciousness. Understand this principle and carry out your life as you like.

September 16, 1979

Maharaj: The flame of Vishnu is supposed to be ever-effulgent and lustrous; because it has entered this body doesn't mean a change in quality. Whether that flame enters into an animal or a human being it does not lose its natural quality. Even if you claim it as your own, saying "I Am," it is still one. The empire of consciousness is yours, and when you realize that, you will know that you are not a person.

Questioner: Maharaj has said that the "I Am" is the consciousness through which comes the world; behind that is awareness, but there is no "I" consciousness. Implicit in the word awareness is this existence; existence also implies proprietorship. That means whose existence is it? One comes back to the feeling of "I."

M: Who is understanding, knowing, your awakened state?

Q: The "I Am."

M: The waking state is "I Amness," but who observes that "I Amness"? Before that waking state, are you not there?

Q: That awareness, or sense of being, has a reference point, and the reference point always has to come back to that which feels its existence as being and "I-ness."

M: There is no proprietor behind that feeling of awareness.

Q: How can you know that?

M: It only is; it is beyond description; words cannot be of any use. That is the permanent state and this manifestation is only its movement. Nobody becomes a Parabrahman, nobody *can* become a Parabrahman; It is. Before the knowledge "I Am" appeared on you, that is Parabrahman.

Q: It's understandable that the "I Am" equates with the ego and mind. Now God, in his own description of Himself says, "I Am That I Am" as being the truth. There are two "I's" involved.

M: One "I" is the substratum and the other is the moving cosmos.

Q: If one reverts back and gets beyond the "I Amness," there still remains a sense of "I."

M: If you revert properly, the consciousness "I Am" will disappear. There is no movement.

Q: Guru has been compared to the sun, in that Guru radiates light, and it is incumbent on the seeker to turn toward that light.

M: Guru is only purest consciousness which is all-pervading.

Q: But the books describe situations in which the sadhaka is looking for his master and it is said that the Guru looks harder and yearns more to find the sadhaka.

M: Don't quote any books here. Ask directly. Don't even use the word Guru—purest consciousness, that's all.

Q: There is a seeker who is seated before this purest consciousness. It is said that the pure consciousness manifests itself personally, as well as impersonally; can he then take a personal interest in the sadhaka, rather than having the sadhaka turn to the light?

M: He is a real seeker who desires to get knowledge of the Self only. The rest of the desires will entitle you to be called jiva and not sadhaka. This is only the kite-flying of your intellect.

Q: Does that mean that the sadhaka before him loves the pure consciousness more than the pure consciousness loves him?

M: They are not two, they are one. There is no difference.

Q: That is on the Absolute plane.

M: If you feel that stream of love flowing, it is your own pure consciousness which is flowing. Don't think that you are loving somebody, or caring for the Guru, or that the Guru must care for you. It is your own Self which is wanting to know and which is flowing with love. That love is the Self loving the Self.

Q: But is it not true that there is something coming from the pure consciousness continually to help realize this?

M: The remembrance of the Guru strikes only those whom the whole pure consciousness is wanting to be one with.

Q: We are led to believe that a pure mind is one of the requisites to achieve Self-realization. By "pure" do we understand auspicious thoughts within that mind, or any thought at all regardless of its content?

M: Throw off the mind completely. It is only the indication of the body-mind consciousness. You are without shape or name. When the water comes out of the river, has it changed in quality? The receptacle of that water is only imagination, water is one. Who is manifesting through all the great incarnations? Who is also manifesting through the donkeys and pigs? All is consciousness only.

September 17, 1979

Questioner: In Western theology there is a great law of sacrifice which has two benefits. If one sacrifices bad habits, not only is their recurrence overcome but willpower is built also. The other benefit of sacrificing bad habits is that when the moment comes to ask for something, surely it will be granted. Does this law hold true with Maharaj also?

Maharaj: This is absolutely correct. Willpower grows and you are granted what you want. Sacrifice is giving up and donating yourself. In higher expression it is called detachment.

Q: Can Maharaj recommend what we might give up initially in order to achieve this end?

M: When you come here I do not take you to be an ordinary person. I assume that you have studied enough before you came here. Therefore I do not tell you openly to leave this or that, because I believe your standard is very high, very much higher; you are not an ordinary seeker. You have a superior intellect; that is why I talk to you like this.

Q: That kind of confidence makes it difficult for me to live up to that standard.

M: I do not ask you to keep up to a certain standard; I only ask you to see what is.

Q: Relating to his question about sacrifice being helpful to attain what one wants: is not wanting itself a habit? Does not wanting come out of ignorance?

M: The raindrops are falling; is it not the nature of the rain to fall, of the wind to blow? To want something is natural, so long as there is the identity with the body-mind. Once that is transcended there will be no wants.

Q: My experience has been that the more I detach from the body-mind, the less I want, and the more my needs are simply fulfilled.

M: Even to think that you are becoming detached is not correct, because you are already detached. When your ego is completely dissolved then you are employing multitudes of bodies.

Q: Knowingly or unknowingly?

M: Everything manifests and there is no individuality. It is all-pervading, it is not necessary to do it knowingly.

Q: It is simply happening? there is no question of knowing or not knowing?

M: Yes. Why does this conflict normally occur? Why the dispute between us? People come here with some profound concepts of spirituality. They think that they have spiritual knowledge, and they want me to give them a clean certificate, "Yes, you are very knowledgeable." This I don't do, I blast their concepts, and hence the confrontation. This is how the disharmony starts.

Q: Yes, it is for this confrontation that I have come here; yet the mind, the thing that holds the concepts, is afraid. Only willpower sustains me.

M: Who is the knower of the willpower?

Q: If Maharaj wants to ask about the knower, the mind can always give an answer, the mind is always capable of giving a concept, but I am now seeing what that is and, as best I can, am making an effort.

M: It's all right. I know that you are identifying with that mind-consciousness, I know it.

Q: I know it too.

M: Try to know that "I."

Q: Yes. When I first came to know that I was coming here, the mind became very excited, with many questions and ideas of what it was like to be with Maharaj, but I saw very clearly that it was the play of the mind. So, for me to come here each morning with questions, for me personally, I know it is the play of the mind. For me it must come in the confrontation.

M: Now that you have understood the quality of the mind have you attained peace?

Q: There have been moments, and then the mind again rambles.

M: You know that you are not the mind. Did you reach that state in which you witness the play of the mind earlier or when you came here?

Q: Earlier, that was a part of the development. Ten years ago something happened to me. From what has been said, what you call Sat Guru appears to be this thing that I have no name for. I have followed that call for ten years. There is no difference between that inner thing and what I am experiencing with Maharaj. I have a question on technique. When one closes the eyes and dwells in the "I Am," initially there is darkness which is observed. It is known that that twilight can be changed into clarity and it will become infinite. How can you achieve that?

M: Why do you want to change it?

Q: If it is within the capability of the one perceiving that darkness to change it into light, why hang about in the darkness? Why not enjoy the light?

M: Who are you to turn it into light? It is in that darkness that several lights of lights are flowing. That is not darkness; it is the pool of nectar. Dive into it. Let it be.

Q: There is another problem encountered in the state of "I Am," that initially the state is felt to be contained in the head itself, and it develops into a tremendous force whose release is actually the spilling over of the consciousness to fill, say, a room. Is this proper?

M: Speak without the body consciousness. That consciousness which you say spills into the room spontaneously occupies the room and the cosmos totally. In the process of stabilizing it expands into the cosmos. When it expands fully, then it stabilizes in the Brahma aperture, the Brahmarandhra.

Q: There are many students of Kundalini Yoga, of Shakti; does the Jnani necessarily, through his practice, through his being, awaken the Kundalini that others speak about?

M: The Jnani has no interest whatsoever in the Kundalini. Prior to your birth where was the Kundalini? This Kundalini is all that you perceive, all that you see. They call it by different names, that's all.

Q: But some Yogis concentrate a force which goes through the seven chakras and presumably follows the spinal column.

M: What you say is correct, but prior to your birth it was not there. It is only thought.

Q: Are they all deluded, then, in pursuing the study of Kundalini Yoga?

M: Anyone who wants to practice anything can do so, but what is it? Zero—nothing.

Q: From what is being said it appears that all of this remains a play in consciousness and if one chooses to identify with consciousness one can play an infinite number of games.

M: Whatever one chooses or likes, he is invited to follow that profession or entertainment.

Q: What we have been doing is trying to find the real game to play and yet it all remains a game in consciousness.

M: You are not playing, you are witnessing.

Q: I have seen that what has kept me playing in consciousness is a fear that nothing will happen. The moments that I have been apparently free from consciousness, things happen anyhow, but they don't arise out of my desire. They happen because the universe pushes them.

M: When you see that, are you in the consciousness?

Q: At least it appears that I am out of it; I see the dream for a dream.

M: You don't know whether you are in it or out of it; you simply witness it.

Q: As long as there is the connection with the body it seems to me that the witness is still in the dream in some way.

M: Yes, he is not awake, it's a dream.

Q: It's like those moments between dream and awakening, when one is suddenly aware that one is dreaming. There is no break in the continuity of one who wakes up in that dream. I am awake in a dream.

M: That dream is yourself. Whatever you see is not the dream, that is the "I" that you are. That consciousness that sees everything sees through the dream itself.

Q: Will the mantra be useful in moments of mental fluctuation?

M: Yes; it is for that only—to check your fluctuating mind.

September 18, 1979

Questioner: In practice I am discovering that there is a subtle difference right now in being the consciousness "I Am." I can meditate "I Am," but there is not the feeling that "I AM." It just seems to be exterior to something.

Maharaj: When you feel that you are separate from the feeling "I Am," isn't there something or someone who knows that there is a difference?

Q: No, it's just a sensation.

M: Find out, are you separate unknowingly.

Q: It feels like an observation.

M: Are we all here because of our own volition to be born or has this knowingness appeared in us unknowingly?

Q: Unknowingly.

M: This beingness has come to you without your knowledge, but you are using it according to your own volition. I want to sentence that individuality to death. Is it not justice that I pronounce this sentence? So think carefully. That individuality must go. Parabrahman is purest justice and Truth.

We are not speaking here today because of our own volition; we think we have a choice, but we don't.

You may achieve samadhi for a day or a month, but when you return to normal the consciousness is not different. You think you have achieved samadhi, but that which thinks this is already there, and has not come by your choice.

Q: Is it possible to lose body consciousness as in samadhi while maintaining "I Amness"?

M: During samadhi that knowingness "I Am" is held in abeyance.

Q: But nothing goes, nothing is lost?

M: No, nothing is lost.

Q: Is this the same thing as "I Am," this will, volition?

M: It is the "I Amness." It appears spontaneously and then it is put to use out of volition.

Witnessing happens to the principle prior to consciousness, to the Absolute, but the Absolute witnesses with the aid of consciousness. In the dream there is no physical "I" present, but still you see. The substratum of everything is that Awareness.

Q: Does the Absolute appear and disappear spontaneously?

M: That state prior to the consciousness is always there. This appearing and disappearing spontaneously is the quality of the consciousness.

Normally the Guru expounds according to the level of the person. Normally he tells the ignorant that on dissolution, or death, everything merges into consciousness. He doesn't talk about the principle prior to consciousness because not all will understand.

Q: Will the Jnani have another dawn after the sun has descended? Can he effect another consciousness?

M: There is no rising or setting for this Jnani principle.

You cannot condition a Jnani by your words; he is the Absolute.

Q: Can there be awareness without consciousness?

M: The Absolute, the Awareness, is the supporting principle for the consciousness.

Q: But awareness of what? Can there be awareness without an object to be aware of?

M: In the Parabrahman state the quality of knowingness is not present, nor does it have any embellishments or decorations like the manifest consciousness. The Parabrahman state does not know it is, neither does it have this manifestation. In spite of the dissolution of universes and cosmos that Absolute is untouched. It exists. That principle is now talking with the aid of consciousness. In the realm of consciousness this manifestation is going on continually.

Q: I used to live on an island and I would often watch the ocean. Waves appeared and disappeared constantly and I realized that this is the concept. That there was no difference in the play of the waves and what I was seeing in the world. That my individuality was only one momentary flash; but my realization remains a description of an experience only.

M: The Absolute is beyond the consciousness which is manifest. That is the play of that dynamic life force, that ocean of knowledge.

Q: Is that principle absent when the waves are still?

M: The Absolute has no connection with this ocean consciousness principle, but without the Absolute it cannot be. The Absolute is the support of the principle.

September 19, 1979

Questioner: I started a course in concentration a few years ago, and after a while it helped me to find the hooks and handles for controlling the mind. I remained with one exercise for some time. It was the mental visualization of an object against a black background, to the exclusion of all else. I understand that the practice of concentration is so powerful that it can change the convolutions of the brain itself. Can I continue that practice and what will be the end result?

Maharaj: Unless you know yourself you will not realize the effects of that concentration, and once you know your Self you will not need the concentration. Whose is the concentration; for what?

Q: The ability to make the mind one-pointed is the precursor to any form of meditation. To be able to still the mind is the cornerstone of any type of realization, because all thoughts must be uprooted before that which is behind them makes itself evident. That's why I chose the study of meditation.

M: Does whatever you want to learn, achieve, or realize come through meditation or concentration? Prior to meditation is some entity already present?

Q: Yes.

M: You are not going to have the birth of that entity through your meditation; it is already present.

Q: I can identify that entity more readily if there are no obtrusive thoughts clouding it.

M: It is only because of all those thoughts that you are not reaching the entity that you desire to reach.

Q: But I am now, only because I have been able to still and control the mind through the practice of concentration.

M: You will find your realization, or understanding, according to whatever meaning you attach to your conceptions or imaginations.

Q: It's generally agreed that meditation is useful in trying to attain the prerequisite sensations. For instance, the meditation on "I am the all-penetrating and infinite light 'I Am'" will lead one to the threshold of the state to which Maharaj is referring.

M: Yes, this meditation is to lead you to be a sadhaka. What are you seeking? Meditation is only an initial state.

Q: But is it an aid?

M: The sadhaka must practice meditation; to reach that particular center which you are seeking meditation is absolutely necessary. The meditator is prior to the meditation.

Q: Last night in my meditation what Maharaj had said about the answer preceding the question came to mind, and I saw that, indeed, the question can only come from having contacted the answer. A problem arose; when Maharaj says that we are not the body, does he mean body as form?

M: Have you any knowledge of how this body come into existence?

Q: The body and awareness came about at the same time; I don't have prior knowledge of the body.

M: You must know why this body came, how this consciousness came on you.

Q: If this question is to be answered truthfully, that is still before me, something which I am seeking to know.

M: You think over only that point, that question. How did this consciousness appear on you?

Q: If the Ultimate Reality is in all the atoms of the universe, is not the body in its very atomic substance the Ultimate Reality?

M: What atom is responsible for this body? Have you an answer?

Q: What is responsible for the body, world, jiva and God is the "I Am." When it arises so do all the others.

M: What next?

Q: The body comes about as a conflux of two fluids; the instructions inherent in those fluids compose the form. That is how the body is derived.

M: The knowledge "I Am" was absent during the nine months in the fetus. That "I Amness" came after the body was born.

Q: No; Maharaj said that the "I Am" was created at the time of conception.

M: At the point of conception did you know that you were present?

Q: No, but that may be due only to my inability then.

M: Until you met your mother did you know anything?

After being indoctrinated you became conscious that you are a body, a son, etc. You did not even remember yourself until then.

Q: That is not consistent with what has been said previously.

M: Whatever was said previously does not pertain to you at all—throw it out. The material for making sugar is in the sugarcane; you take the sugar and throw the cane out. Similarly, whatever is said now is the sugar which has been derived from the cane. That sweetness has neither name nor form. You know it, I know it, this taste of sweetness that you are. What is going to happen to that taste?

Q: I go on tasting.

M: That taste is not everlasting, that taste will not last. Once you understand this, what is your future?

Q: The future remains a mystery.

M: Can that sweetness have a mystery?

Q: That sweetness will eventually disappear, so the mystery can't be in the sweetness. The taste is not the mystery, the taster is the mystery. Is consciousness the taster?

M: You know that. You know the answer. The taste is of the five elements. The source of the body is the five elements; you are not the body. The combination of the body and the vital breath generates this consciousness; you are not the consciousness. You are the underlying principle. Be in That.

Q: To be here and hear Maharaj repeat it over and over is quite a different matter from suddenly confronting it directly; and in that moment of first confrontation one is not completely clear.

M: Who is to confront whom? It is all thoughts. You have understood something and you can't admit that you have understood; so keep quiet, be in that.

M: Where are you coming from? *(To another:)* You.

Q: I am coming from Ramanasram.

M: Are you having good samadhan there?

Q: If samadhan means inner peace, yes, very much so.

M: If a liquid is boiled to remove the impurities in it the condition when bubbles cease to rise is called samadhan. So long as there is any vritti [movement] in the mind it is not samadhan.

Q: I am still getting some bubbles! The deeper my dhyana [meditation, contemplation], the weaker and more painful is my body. The condition distracts my mind. Would Maharaj suggest something?

M: For some time such conditions may appear. Even Ramana Maharshi had some suffering at one time in the body [burning sensation]. Don't be afraid of them. Gently continue your meditation, study, and nama smaranam [remembrance of the name]. In sadhana each one's experience will be different due to the differences in the prakriti [nature] and gunas [qualities] of the instrument.

Q: I request Maharaj to bless me with the necessary courage and inner strength to ignore the body and mind.

M: With full unshakable faith in Ramana Maharshi continue your practice. You can come here and listen to me, but remember that your Sat Guru is Ramana Maharshi.

Q: I am returning to Ramanasram tomorrow; would Maharaj give me something of his as prasad that I can keep with me?

M: My prasad for you is this: that you should have Purna, Nishta Bhakti [full, unshakable devotion] to your Guru Ramana Maharshi, come what may. Rain or shine, pleasure or pain, life or death, your faith should not be shaken. You don't have to go anywhere or see any other Saints. He is your Guru.

Q: Would Maharaj tell us what is the benefit of being here in his presence.

M: It cannot be measured. You cannot measure space, and, similarly, the good fortune of having a Sat Guru is immeasurable. If you can understand that you are fortunate.

Q: Before coming here I thought that my heart was cold, but now I find that it is defrosting in the presence of the Great Defroster.

M: Let anything come and go. You are only a witness. Don't get wounded or involved in this melting process; it is only on the mental level and different from your Self. Whatever experience is derived through the mind cannot affect you. You are beyond mental cognition, beyond the five elements. The mind is made of those elements only.

September 20, 1979

Questioner: What are virtue and faith?

Maharaj: Virtue is what you possess when you know what you are and live in that knowledge. Knowing Truth you must act.

Q: Virtue is behavior then, and it comes as a blessing from the Sage, rather than something one can acquire. Similarly, faith is required for Self realization and it also comes as a gift from the Sage. Would Maharaj comment on these two statements?

M: What you have said is correct, and it is said for the good of an individual's behavior; but what I say is only about the universal manifestation and not about a personality.

Q: Maharaj has mentioned, on occasion, an advanced soul. Observation has it that all souls are similar; there is neither superiority nor inferiority, but rather there is the feeling of the brotherhood of all mankind.

M: We are intimately connected with all the universal scene. That universal brotherhood is present in every atom, whether in the food or in your body. When my individuality is given up, dissolved, my body and all the activities become universal; they are of universal use. There is no claiming any action out of it as "mine".

Q: Maharaj didn't quite answer my question.

M: You are asking as an individual and I am replying from the manifest principle. As for how an individual should behave with others, there are different schools.

Q: Yesterday a question was asked about the efficacy of fasting and Maharaj gave an individual answer.

M: The answer was for the ignorant and not the advanced seeker.

Q: I was seeking aids which would help toward Self realization.

M: There is no question of Self realization. That "you" realizes everything, experiences everything, witnesses everything. You are prior to that. Whatever deep conviction you hold onto in the core of you will happen.

Q: The questions that I ask, aside from the major ones which have already been answered, are the small brush strokes which give the final touch to the painting.

M: When you have become the very soul of all the souls, is it necessary that you should seek the help of others on how to apply the finishing touches? You don't depend on anybody, everything depends on your conviction that you are. The picture is complete now. You have come to get your recognition. Your recognition abides in the Self.

Q: This is a new experience, a new adjustment.

M: It is not new at all. It is most ancient and eternal.

Q: I know, I know! It is said that we should surrender; what do we surrender?

M: Ourselves we surrender, not only our possessions. We surrender the entire knowledge. There are various types of charity, but the greatest charity is the renunciation of the knowledge "I am." When you give that up you escape birth and death.

Q: How should we move in the world?

M: Just leave off moving. You are doing nothing. Waking state represents activity, deep sleep represents peace, quiet. When these two are present it means "I Am" is there, but you, the Absolute are neither the waking state, deep sleep, nor "I Amness."

Q: Why do I feel only this body as me, a particular body as mine?

M: Stop thinking about that body; take hold only of the waking and deep sleep as you.

Q: How can I eliminate the fear of death?

M: Because you have faith in death you are pampering it. Do not ask any questions for fifteen days; listen quietly to the questions and the answers. All your questions will be answered automatically. Just keep quiet.

Among all this crowd, if one should open up that is good enough for me. This is the last step, from beingness to nobeingness. Whatever the acquisitions or accumulations of the last millions of births, they will be exploded here.

Q: At lunch yesterday some of us were commenting on that very fact. This is a unique and ideal place wherein you can bring something and get lots of nothing in return.

M: Very apt. The totality of nothingness.

Q: I have a question. Would a dog know that he is a dog or would he just know "I Am"?

M: It is you that call him a dog; he does not know that he is a dog.

Q: Do dogs have a sensation "I am hungry" when they are hungry or just a sensation of hunger? The reason I ask is that a famous Yogi said that most animals just have an awareness of hunger, they have no "I Amness."

M: He knows. Even animals know. His only identity is body. He knows it by his body; therefore he always tries to protect his own body, just as birds, insects and human beings protect their bodies to preserve their "I Amness."

Q: People who practice meditation apparently reach other levels of consciousness within the "I." Are these levels as real as the three primary states, or are they a creation of the mind?

M: Know that knowingness only! Your beingness is like a tape recorder or a film in which all this has already been recorded and is being projected in the waking state, sleep, meditation or whatever, but the primary condition is the "I" consciousness. When you get this Self knowledge and abide in the quietude, you will realize that all the universes are already present in this atomic consciousness. All this knowledge is word-ly knowledge, but you have to understand, to realize that.

At present you have the knowledge of the words that have been given to you about that beingness, but when you abide in the beingness you will realize that all is the play of consciousness. When you realize that it is already recorded in that consciousness of yours, you will discard it. That consciousness is disposable.

The "I" is full of desires; instead of trying to fulfill the desires, find out what this "I" is. Understand desire. Nothing in the world has any attraction for me. If someone brings me gold or diamonds I will tell him to take them away. What good are they to me, I can't eat them. For me, the memory of my Guru is the most precious. I did not even bother about the power of doing miracles. For those powers you have to follow certain rituals, certain disciplines.

Q: The Sage then has no siddhis [powers] because he didn't observe those rituals?

M: A Jnani does not seek powers because he has recognized that that atomic consciousness contains it all. It is multi-energy, multi-power, and he has already discarded it.

Q: Does Maharaj follow a lineage of Navanath?

M: I follow all variations.

Q: Does Maharaj consider himself as following in the footsteps of his Guru?

M: He has no footsteps. He has no feet.

September 21, 1979

Questioner: If all manifestation is considered illusion, how does it differ from thought?

Maharaj: It is only for worldly activity that the distinction is made; it is all the same.

Q: When one says he is free from thought, he can be free from intellectual meditation, but if his eyes are open the illusion persists. Is that free from thought?

M: Take out the word illusion and substitute the word Brahma. It is only the words you can change, nothing else.

You go to a Jnani for knowledge, but of what are you seeking knowledge, and who is it that seeks knowledge? The knowledge you are seeking is about Maya, or illusion, but you will not give adequate attention to who it is who wants the knowledge.

Q: The Sage is the one who can clarify all questions, be they relative or absolute, and that is why such questions are put to the Sage.

M: When you put questions do you feel that they will solve your problems? Are you asking them from the content of the question, and are you keeping your Self in view when you ask?

Q: What is perplexing to me now is the individual's comportment in life after leaving here. I am concerned as to how the mind will fend for itself in supporting the body and its activities.

M: When the mind becomes absolutely purified it will look after everything.

Q: I understand, but it is the wait until the purification occurs that distracts me.

M: So long as the vital breath is flowing the mind will be flowing.

Q: I seem to be coming to a bifurcation in the road and that's why. . . .

M: I am only telling you that this body, vital breath, and consciousness are one, and you are beyond it. Your mind will decide how you should behave when you go back. Let the body and mind work according to their own inclinations, and the conditions, but know you are not them.

Q: I was wondering whether I should find a tropical island somewhere and sit under a tree and absorb this or go back into society and continue what I did before.

M: Are you going to purify your body or your vital breath?

Q: Right.

M: If you think that this talk is stupid, throw it out and do what you like. I don't insist that you should listen to me and abide by my words.

Q: I have understood what Maharaj has been saying, and he has been repeating it in several different fashions. I understand!

M: What else is there except that touch of "I Am"? Why do you worry about discovering Maya and Brahma and all that? Understand what this principle "I Am" is and you are finished. That "I Am" is in bondage because of concepts.

Q: Returning to the relative state: should I go back to the activity in which I was engaged before coming here?

M: That person, does it relate to the body, the vital breath, or the "I Am"?

Q: The body.

M: How are you, the witness of these three entities, concerned? They can carry on the work for thousands of years; in what way are you concerned? The question arose because you are considering the body which will decompose and decay when the vital breath leaves it. You are identifying with and embracing that body.

Q: Yes.

M: Your nearest relatives, including your wife and son, will not approach that body when it decomposes.

Q: That's quite true.

M: Having understood, carry on your business. Don't worry.

It is said that when Rama wanted to cross over the sea from India to Lanka, the monkeys helped him quite a bit. Therefore he blessed them all with heaven. Those same monkeys have come to enjoy themselves now in the Western countries. They are enjoying the boon of material and heavenly pleasure that Rama gave. The Rishis who have done a lot of penance with the intention of gaining heaven are also born there and enjoy themselves. Now they have had enough and have started coming here in order to search for Rama again.

September 22, 1979

Maharaj: No great man having taken birth has wrought an iota of change in the consciousness. What is, is; it will never change. You just have to see and know; no action or ritual is called for. Unknowingly this knowingness has appeared in you, and you have to go through it, willingly or unwillingly. The experience is there and somebody comes later to experience it.

No one can change what he has to face as experience so long as he is identifying with the body and mind. When there are floods or fires, loss or gain, you just have to accept them. That is consciousness working.

Questioner: I had an interesting experience last night. I was sitting alone, enjoying my dinner, when a very boorish man with his family of five came in and commandeered my table, telling me that I should not have the table to myself. I felt like hitting the guy. What is one supposed to do?

M: You must restrain yourself as much as possible.

Q: It would not have been the body restraining itself.

M: The body does nothing. The body is protected by the vital breath and that quality of beingness. Vital breath is responsible for all movement, and the quality of beingness sits on a high pedestal and watches.

Q: Is there a state where you feel that beingness is unrelated to the body?

M: Why don't you steady yourself in that beingness. Forget the body sense, and what remains is only you, Turiya [Super-conscious state].

Q: I have faith that I am everything—there is nothing else—but it only comes rarely and for a short time.

M: Even when you witness that everything is you, it is still the quality of the five elemental body and will not last. Waking state, deep sleep, and this Turiya—all these are temporary states.

Q: Then what is eternal?

M: That One which you have not forgotten. That Eternal state is beyond the state of remembering and forgetting.

Q: Where is the proof?

M: At that stage, whatever the principle is that is demanding proof, only that principle remains. In that state there is nothing; so where is the question of producing proof and for whom?

Q: What I meant is: at what stage do you feel that you have it?

M: There is nobody else, there is you only. What you are doing is trying to identify with God, but God can't be unless you are.

Q: I don't believe in God.

M: If you don't believe in God, do you believe in body? Who rejects God? Who is that?

Q: Me.

M: What is that "me"?

Q: It is just a feeling.

M: You are God; if God is not, you are not. If God is, you are.

Q: When Christ said that He and the Father were one, was He referring to His father as Iswara and not as the Supreme Being?

M: The one whose actions are responsible for the beingness is the father.

Q: Christ was not referring to a physical being as the Father?

M: I would not like to decide that. Since Christ was there, the beingness was sustained by the food body. Christ is a great Sage; don't involve yourself in His ancestry. Meditate on Him, be yourself sanctified with His memory; in the process you will be purified. No form will be left of you.

Q: In Western tradition there have been many Saints and Sages who have cured people of various afflictions. The Eastern Sage tends not to get involved in healing. Why is that?

M: An Eastern Sage also has powers to perform miracles. In the process of curing people, naturally his status would be elevated and he would be held in high esteem by society, with the result there is the chance that he will develop pride.

Q: But there is no one there to feel pride.

M: Don't get involved in concepts; it will strangle you. Rarely some Sage can perform miracles and not feel pride.

Q: The Sage does not have pride. Who is there to have pride?

M: All the activities of this manifest world are through the consciousness. You are imagining a Sage with a body.

This beingness is contained in all the five elements, but it is not personal, it is universal. If you go to sleep with the knowledge that you are consciousness, that same thought will prevail through the day. Sleep with the conviction that the body is space. It is the thought that you are the body that brings suffering. Keep in mind, every day, that you are not the body, that you are simply the knowledge, the consciousness. After my death my body will be transformed into space; so why not presume that it is the space now?

Q: This is adding more concepts.

M: I am getting rid of the concept that you are the body. Why do you say that I am adding more concepts?

Q: To say that my body is space is another concept.

M: The very soul of all concepts is "I Am."

Q: To think "I am space" before going to sleep is a technique.

M: You had better quit and tell everyone that you came across a fool and that he would have hanged you, but somehow you saved yourself. I was telling you the nature of that consciousness; I want to gradually make you free from all concepts. Just by saying that everything is a concept does not free you. You will merely go from a gross concept to a subtler one. When you are entertaining gross concepts such as "I am the body," they multiply into more concepts: "My body is ill," "I must take pills," "I must see a doctor," etc. Suppose you say, "I am space"; what further concept can you have?

I want to take you to that "I Am" concept which is the last outpost of illusion and get rid of it. Understand the quality of these concepts.

Q: I have a question. Earlier Maharaj said that attentiveness should always be present. Can attentiveness be experienced as a feeling? Feeling seems to be prior to the knowing. There is an underlying sensation of always knowing that I am. Is that equal to perceiving, witnessing?

M: The feeling is the same as attention. When you are aware "I am the seer, I am the knower," that simply is, and It has no shape. That knowledge is formless; when you embrace the form the problems arise.

September 23, 1979

Maharaj: I expect nothing of you, I make myself freely available to you. If an ignorant person understands and imbibes what I say he will be liberated. Why? Because of faith in the Guru, in the precious words of the Guru. People who depend on the intellect only always will be swinging like a pendulum. Imbibe fully whatever I have told you, make it your own. There is no question of any aids or discipline; by your firm conviction alone you transcend everything.

What capital is available to you? Only that "I Am"; it is a product of the five-elemental food essence. First you become this consciousness; then you realize that you are the manifestation.

Because this body is created out of this gross earth, vegetation, etc., it is the receptacle of all dirt and disease, but this very body can be put to proper use for realization if you depend for guidance on the words of the Guru. The one who realizes the Self, his place becomes a place of pilgrimage for many afterwards. Just like Sai Baba, people go and worship his statue and their prayers are answered. What is that statue? It is made of rock.

Whatever my Guru said, I implicitly followed, with full conviction, and with that conviction I got results.

You must have the firm conviction that the highest God,

or the Deity, is the knowledge "I Am," but you must get these words from a Guru who is himself a Jnani, the one who has recognized and transcended this knowledge "I Am."

The Bhagavad-Gita says that we have five senses of knowledge; these are very subtle. More subtle than the senses is the mind, more subtle than the mind is the intellect, and subtler than these is the vital breath. And yet more subtle is "He," the beingness, the "I Am."

The Absolute is not these entities. You are the Absolute.

Questioner: I am not able to understand what Maharaj is saying.

M: You know you are sitting here. Be attentive to that knowledge only. Just be in your beingness. That knowingness "I Am" has created the entire universe. Hold on to that; nothing has to be done. Once you recognize that principle it becomes tranquil. Become one with that and all your needs will be satisfied.

At no stage forget that principle; whatever you are doing your attention should be there. When you are eating food, who is eating? Only that beingness. Whatever you are doing is the beingness; pay attention to that beingness.

Q: When I am very attentive to what is being translated the "I Am" seems to disappear, there is no thought arising in me.

M: Are you happy with that?

Q: There is neither happiness nor unhappiness. I am simply tranquil and witnessing; no feeling is involved.

M: Do you understand it or are you merely intellectually wrestling with yourself?

Q: I am not wrestling.

M: Are you at peace with yourself? That is the ultimate criterion.

Q: Not all the time. When I am not attentive to it I get involved.

M: Who is it that says this?

Q: That knowingness only comes afterward. Yesterday a lot of emotion came out; I was blinded by it. While it was happening I was not aware that I was not that.

M: At the time of the emotions you were one with the emotion—you were not witnessing.

Q: Would an enlightened being be involved in that sense, or would he be watching?

M: Your beingness is one—it doesn't become one or the other—but because that beingness has identified itself with your body-mind emotions, the trouble starts. Keep that consciousness separate; then you will not be involved.

Q: After an emotional outburst why is there something like a cleansing feeling?

M: That was a temporary state of mind. When that state of mind disappears you go back to your natural peaceful state.

A Yogi has a trick by which he is out of this misery and happiness. He holds the vital breath in abeyance, but the problem is not solved; it is a state.

You have all the senses and the mental factor. You have to understand the function of each and put it to proper use. Don't say that you are not going to use it, don't keep it out of function. Use it fully because sustenance is to be obtained through it. You must understand that you are not involved in it; you are only a witness.

If you want to become a king you must have your subjects, an army, and an administration. Similarly, to become a Jnani you must have this paraphernalia and understand it; only then do you rule.

Q: Do the three states—witnessing, Iswara conciousness, and the Absolute—happen at the same time?

M: This is the actual state of affairs. Today you feel that you are the body; give that idea up. "I am this manifestation only"; be there. You are the manifest Bhagavan, Iswara principle. It is a simple meditation. You start scratching and continue to scratch until the blood comes; that is the intellectual wrestling. Just be still. Let it settle down. Don't dig up questions.

I have been very open, very explicit. I've been telling you that you are not the body, you are the knowledge only, and this vital breath is your conveyance, a tool by which you carry out your activities, and the knowledge "I Am" is very subtle. Because of your knowledge, you are and the world is.

I am inclined to think that in future I must say, "A thousand rupees cash down to listen to my talks." Only then will you be serious. I should charge you a thousand rupees and give the entire course in one day; what is the use of your staying here for a month? When you charge for something it becomes very precious.

Q: In the past people used to give kingdoms for this knowledge.

M: There were so many disciplines, they had to live in the forest and live on berries and fruit; they could not store food. Those were the conditions.

September 25, 1979

Questioner: It's very hard to convince myself that I am the "I Am"; there is always the little feeling inside that I am beyond it. So how can I embrace the "I Am" totally?

Maharaj: Don't employ the words. It is like a seed that has been planted and that you have to water every day for three months before the sprouting takes place. What you have heard should subside inside; it must be assimilated. This is all word-ly knowledge. Just watch.

You are coming here from an ashram?

Q: Yes.

M: Do you have faith in your Guru?

Q: Yes, I have faith in him.

M: Why leave that Guru and wander around like this? You must go to him only.

Q: I am still not satisfied; I have a lot of reservations.

M: If you have reservations, it is best that you leave him; otherwise completely surrender yourself—doubts and convictions, everything.

If you have accepted one Guru, implicit faith—and complete surrender—is very necessary. Serving the Guru is following whatever guidance he gives you through words. You must imbibe and become one with those words.

Before you surrender to any Guru you are free to move anywhere, a free-lance spiritual seeker. Go anywhere, collect spiritual information, do what you like; but once you accept a Guru there must be complete surrender.

Don't think that the Guru is some person; it is not so. The Guru is that beingness, and beingness is manifestation. All the world is beingness and that is the Guru.

Q: Does this hold true if one has a Guru who is no longer embodied? Maharaj has said that if one has surrendered to a Guru one should not shop around.

M: If that Guru was no more how could you experience the world? The one who recognizes this beingness and transcends it is Sat Guru. Otherwise there are Gurus who are just shopkeepers, trading in spirituality.

Q: When Maharaj speaks Absolutely, am I identical to Maharaj or am I equivalent?

M: We are one. Abide in the words of the Guru. This disciple is obsessed by the concept which is standing on his shoulders. My Guru gave this same knowledge to various disciples, but the behavior of each disciple is different. Each has a different concept about what the Guru has said, and he hangs onto the personal concept which he likes the most.

Try to understand the significance of the "I Am." The more you try to gauge, the higher you will find the quality. Don't belittle yourself. You are not a man or a woman; you are that principle out of which all has come.

Q: Yesterday I was inhering in this "I Am" state off and on, and gemstones came to my mental vision. They were so clear: they shone with a dark amber color, very beautiful.

M: They are the precious stones of the knowledge. The stones are radiating out of the knowledge. If they shine on others they will be liberated; such are those precious ones. In spite of my indicating to you what you are, you are still hanging on to the body and embracing death.

Q: What does Maharaj mean by "shine on others"?

M: Does the sun ask whether my light will shine on others? Have you confirmed who you are?

Q: I find the concept that I am the sun difficult.

M: Be without any concepts. Confirm that you are not the body.

Q: How do I develop love for others?

M: Don't try to love somebody, be love. When you are love, that love will be useful to humanity. Just like water, if you are water, everything will grow.

Q: Christ said that we should love others as the Self.

M: Everything is your Self, there is no other. All this is the expression of your love.

I am not going to hammer in the same guiding words again and again. You absorb it.

September 26, 1979

Questioner: I had an experience early this morning. I awakened and sat for meditation for forty minutes. There were vibration-type things in my head, nothing but bliss; there were no visions. I was the center and I had the sense of "I-I," one on top of another. When I started coming back into duality I heard cymbals, and into my perception comes Maharaj dancing, playing the cymbals. I said to him, "We are in the middle of a forest; do you have to play those things all the time?" He continued playing and dancing but there was no longer any sound.

Maharaj: After having this experience would you like to ask something?

Q: No.

M: Experiences take rise in the beingness and in that knowledge again they merge.

Q: There was the experience "I Am," but another was imposed on it, an attraction to get behind the "I Am."

M: If the sun can enter into its own light then you can go behind your beingness. You are the one who knows "I Am." All these experiences flow out of your beingness. There is no gain and no loss out of the experiences. They do not affect you. That beingness will get to that spiritual path when it is in earnest to do so, but so long as a vestige of body identity persists it will fail.

All of you want experiences, but they will not fill you. If the consciousness is getting restless to know the Self it will throw away everything and run to the goal. That is my own experience.

Hundreds and thousands of local people and foreigners have been here. They have become my disciples and gone. I have invited none of them; it is the hunger of their own soul which brought them here.

Out of the hunger and earnestness of my own soul I came to know my own Self to such an extent that Bhagavan Krishna's philosophy became mine. This Krishna consciousness is my Self, yet I am out of it. Everything is in me, is resting on me.

The Absolute is Paramatman. From this total Reality comes the chidakasha, the wanting to be. From there the physical space, the entire manifestation, comes into being in a fraction of a second. In deep sleep there is nothing, then there is the slightest feeling that I want to be awake, then the entire manifestation takes place within a split second. The manifest has appeared on the Unmanifest and movement started, but the witness is the Absolute.

The experiences that you have—do they give you anything? Are you trying to understand the central point? We call what has happened to you a vision, and that vision is always within the sight.

Q: When I first had this experience I was aware of the witness aspect. When I experienced the sensation "I-I", I asked myself to whom it had come, and it disappeared.

M: Was this temporary or are you in it all through the day?

Q: I am now. The continuation of that feeling I had this morning—there is something within me that is pulling me and at the same time giving me an abstract feeling. It is just very easy for me, right now, to go into the "I Am." There is a definite feeling that permeates the head as well as the chest, and I can be gone very quickly.

M: You are awake and are seeing the world and the witnessing of your being awake and seeing the world is taking place. How simple this is: in the waking state I am so and so, and this waking state is the witness. When this waking state goes to sleep that awareness is still there. You are the light behind the states. Krishna gave this knowledge to Arjuna. The one who listened to the knowledge wrote; so what has been given is secondhand knowledge written by a third person.

Whether a Vedantist or a novelist writes, it is only through his own concepts. A novelist writes whatever comes into his imagination; most of it is rubbish, trash, which should not have been written. All that dirt within himself has come out. Whatever you had inside yourself during your waking state exhibited itself in that experience you had.

Q: Do you mean that there is a purification process going on, that more dirt will be coming out?

M: You are not the body. Whatever comes and goes is merely projections of the mind or consciousness.

Q: If there is the likelihood of these things coming out now, should I be concerned?

M: Everything which you have heard, every piece of knowledge, every incident in your life, even if you think that you have forgotten, that consciousness has recorded. Every second that consciousness is registering what you are going through. All the five senses are typing incessantly. You can go further and further, getting into deeper and deeper water, pondering over this, but you should go back, reverse, to the source. Where did you come from? Go back to the source, take your stand in your original state.

My dear, you have understood everything, now use it. Stabilize yourself and go.

September 27, 1979

Maharaj: When I feel that they have sufficient knowledge on which they can continue their own search I tell them to leave. You have allowed that knowledge to sink within your consciousness, but that knowledge will require complete rest. This would be available to you in an ashram. There are several good ones in India.

Questioner: The only ashram I want to be in is the island of the heart.

M: You have achieved it, but it is not necessary that you should be physically present here. You have that island in your possession. I tell you in a very simple way, in a few words, what you should receive, and if you really try to imbibe it, it's over.

For the newcomers there is no room; I have such a small place.

Q: Suppose one wanted to stay for devotional purposes?

M: Provided we have the room. Once you catch hold of that principle which moves about in various disguises there is an end of illusion. This principle, this consciousness, you will see as a snake, then as a buffalo, then as something else. Once you catch hold of the principle you understand.

We are only concerned with that; don't worry about Mahatmas, only this being. Find out that principle. Don't get carried away by the word-ly knowledge. Imbibe the meaning of what I have told you. Go to that Source.

Q: When one actively becomes a witness, quietly observes all that is going on, it does take concentration and it does affect the brain in itself; so you get tired after a while. Similarly, in meditation I cannot stay in the "I Am" stage for longer than thirty or forty minutes. Then the brain seems to vibrate and I have to return back to the normal condition. Will this get better or are there any steps to be taken to get rid of the strain on the brain?

M: Why are you dabbling in this? You know that you are sitting here, I know that you are sitting here. Who witnesses that you are sitting?

Q: The "I Am."

M: Consciousness is sitting, who witnesses sitting? I know you are sitting here, you know that you are sitting; it is completely open, yet very mysterious at the same time. Don't put in special efforts to witness, just be in a relaxed condition. You are studying your mind movements at mind level.

Q: Yes, that's what I am doing.

M: You are practicing witnessing, you are not being the witness. There is no special effort to be made; it just takes place. About concentration: it is something like running around trying to take a photograph of the government of Bombay. Can you take a photograph of the government?

Q: It is difficult to perceive the all.

M: The same government can put handcuffs on you.

Q: Why do I have the feeling after I come down from meditation that there has been some activity and strain on the brain?

M: That "you" that goes into meditation and comes down—describe him. Why do you follow these exercises? Give them up. Just be relaxed in your natural state; that is the highest state. The lower state is concentration and meditation.

Don't get involved in anything, stay in the consciousness "I Am" and don't go on an intellectual binge again.

Consciousness indicates to the consciousness, expounds the knowledge; but you will not dwell there, you embrace this body. The knowledge "I Am" tells the knowledge about itself to the "I Am" only. There is no question of others. "You" and "me" is in reference to the bodies. So we will keep quiet, for nobody is there. All quiet on the front.

Q: About the purification of the mind—what will be taking place?

M: Repeat the mantra that was given; from that the mind gets purified.

Q: Should the mantra be said in conjunction with inhaling and exhaling?

M: Rhythmic, yes. It is the same breath that is going on all the time, but you combine it with the mantra, that's all.

You sit here, and I talk for some time, and then I tell you to go. Just as a mother takes care of a child; then after some time she tells it to go and play outside. It is not that the mother does not want the child; she loves the child. The Guru expounds knowledge to the disciple and takes him out of the body-mind sense, and then asks him to fend for himself.

This beingness is the child of that no-beingness, Absolute state; when the beingness understands the beingness, it attains no-being. Then it does not bother about what happens to this beingness. First you get rid of this world, then you get rid of beingness.

Actually this is the natural state, but we cling to the body and all the trouble starts. When you do not experience the body there are no desires or needs, but when you think you are the body you want to satisfy your desires, thinking that then you will have peace. There is no peace in the body identity.

Q: If one's occupation is being a writer, who does the writing?

M: The chemical, the "I Am" consciousness; it is all a play of consciousness.

Q: Maharaj has stated that when the time is propitious an explosion occurs within the mind that is directly antecedent to the experience of pure being. Could he enlarge on that?

M: It is the floodgates of Truth opening. Having cut off the rope, he broke the shell open. The family normally keeps a clay pot to hold buttermilk and butter. The pot is the shell and is hung from the ceiling by ropes. Having thrown open the door, he cut off the rope [the shackles], broke open the shell [the body], threw out the buttermilk and swallowed the butter [the essence], the knowledge "I Am." After that what is there? Neither "I" nor "you."

Q: Maharaj also says that there is an incident which provokes this mechanism and that it has to be recognized or it will go by and you will have to wait for another incident.

M: Don't worry about that incident prior to the explosion or about anything. You are worrying because of the intellect, but you have only to continue in that "I Am" with faith; you have nothing else to do. You are likely to miss that incident if you try to use your intellect. Just let it happen. Hold on to the feeling "I Am," don't pollute that state by holding on to the body sense.

Q: Maharaj has said that if one dwells on the type of information needed, all the information will flow from it. How does this work?

M: Chemical does it.

Q: Can one enhance that activity in any way?

M: You are enhancing it by coming here.

October 2, 1979

Questioner: What is the witness? Is it the mind or something beyond the mind?

Maharaj: It is the knower of the mind.

Q: If I say "I Am," is that the mind?

M: Beingness expresses through the mind with the words "I Am."

Q: In the books translated by Mr. Frydman the words destiny and justice are used. Are these the same as karma?

M: Justice is the decision given. Destiny is the storehouse out of which all this manifestation flows. It is the principle out of which you have emanated. It is something like the negative of a film; consciousness is already present in that source from which you have emanated, so the film is being projected. What is to be projected is already recorded; so whatever activities happen through that beingness—which is you—are your destiny. Every action, or every step, which that beingness will take is already registered in the film.

Q: Do the stars show that negative, as some astrologers claim?

M: It is a direct perjury. Nine months prior to your birth the destiny was created.

Q: By whom?

M: Nobody; it just happens.

Q: The negative exists before the destiny starts. Where is the negative printed?

M: That is the skill of Mula-Maya [primary illusion].

Q: Some people believe that as they sow, so shall they reap, so that somewhere before they have sown the structure of the negative.

M: That is only hearsay; do you have evidence of it?

Q: No.

M: Maya is the primary source of illusion. At that point love for the Self begins; "I Am," the love to be. Its expression is all this manifestation.

Q: Why do some people have more love for this false self than others?

M: There is no question of one loving more than another; the state of love is present, and you have to enjoy or suffer it. Even when we suffer we love our beingness.

Q: When you practice witnessing, is it consciously?

M: What do you mean by practicing witnessing? What you are trying to do is intensify your own beingness. Witnessing will happen automatically, but the Self must open up. Prior to witnessing you are.

Q: Maharaj said to quiet down, but my life style makes it difficult to be quiet; my job has a lot of pressure and activity. Does Maharaj recommend getting a different job?

M: I don't say do this or that. Do what you like; just know that you are not the doer, it is just happening. The destiny that has come into existence on the first day of conception is unfolding itself. There is nothing that you can claim the doership of. Once you know who you are, that destiny does not bind you.

Q: What do people who die do to realize that they don't have a body?

M: Nothing happens, nobody is dead. The texts say that those who die with undissolved concepts will be reborn.

Q: When they are reborn, do they have choices of different bodies, such as going into family A or family B?

M: Why do you bother yourself with such extraneous matters? Concentrate on convincing yourself that you are not the body. This body is made of the five elements and is really a food body; you have no part in it. You are not concerned with this food body. Strength, the breath, and the beingness are dependent on food and water. Without food and water the "I Amness" is absent.

Q: Then does the "I Amness" come back again later?

M: You are none of these things. There is no question of rebirth.

Q: It seems that something called food is floating around in the air. You can make a body out of it, and if you have some wrong concepts you'll land in that food body. Actually implicit in the teaching, it seems to me, is that there really isn't such a thing as food and a food body; that's only a concept.

M: From what level are you talking now? How do you understand that the body is not there, that it comes from the mind?

Q: I'm getting that from what Maharaj says in the book.

M: Have you realized it?

Q: If I had realized it I would be a Jnani.

M: Exactly. Until then the body is born the way every body is born.

Q: Is the way things are for us now that we have a concept of a body which we should accept and not create another concept that there is not a body?

M: Go to the source. Who knows that there is a body? Something is prior to the creation of the body.

Q: Do all the efforts that we make in this regard have any effect in destroying the sense of "I Am," or is that part of the film? So the effort that people think they are making to reach the goal has no effect, it is just all contained in that film?

M: Be in that source which is the light behind consciousness. You are not the consciousness, understand that. What is happening is in that Mula-Maya.

The cassette records what I am saying, but whatever is recorded in the cassette is not me. Just as the original voice is not in the cassette, so you are separate from the chemical, the body, the "I Amness," the consciousness.

Q: Is the realization in the film?

M: It cannot be in the film because you are the knower of the film. Now ponder whatever you have heard and come back at five o'clock.

That mind is only an accumulation of the thoughts that are present in the manifestation. All your activities depend on the mind, and mind depends on all your memories and whatever you have heard in this world.

We are absorbing whatever happens in this world, and we are also looking at it from our own point of view, putting our own concepts on those things. And because this body-mind consciousness absorbs all that happens in the world, we go on crediting this "I Am" consciousness with previous births, birth, karma, etc. You accept certain things as good and virtuous, and reject other as bad or sinful, but these are only the concepts you have acquired in the world, and there is no basis for the distinction.

Q: Yesterday Maharaj spoke of the chakras [centers of psychic energy in the body], and the Brahma-randhra. I wondered if we should be concerned with them in our meditation.

M: Forget about chakras. Catch hold of the knowledge "I Am" and become one with it; this is meditation.

Q: Who is to catch hold of the "I Am"?

M: Who is asking this question?

Q: Are we able to go beyond our thoughts, or, in the Absolute, are the thoughts just part of the film, and if they are, do we just have to bear with them?

M: Who wants to go beyond thought? Who is he? Before consciousness appears in the waking state, that is the Absolute; as soon as the consciousness appears the thoughts come. You do not have to bear with them, nor discard them; simply know them.

Q: All the other things that determine who you call the original—those things do not exist?

M: But that is only when you reach that original stage, when you are a Jnani.

Q: We are already that.

M: If you knew it there would be no questions, and you would not be here.

October 3, 1979

Questioner: The film which Maharaj was speaking of yesterday: I was wondering whether when we inquire, "Who am I?" the answer is the idea of whatever is going on in the film. That is, "Who am I?" and "Who is doing this?" are linked together in the film. Is this correct?

Maharaj: Ever since the beingness has appeared on you, whatever is being done through that knowledge is entirely the result of the five elements working through you and through whatever knowledge of "I Am" you have received out of those elements. "I Am" is prior to the "knowledge I Am," but that which is working through the knowledge, at the moment—that personality which you have taken to yourself—is the result of the essence of the food which comes out of the five elements. Unless you are absolutely quiet and stabilize yourself in the "knowledge I Am" this result of the worldly activities will get separated from "I Am." You must stabilize there first.

Q: Is the witness part of the film witnessing part of the film?

M: As soon as the "I Am" appears on you when you

awake, that is the witness, but after that moment the whole manifestation comes within the view of the "I Am," and he witnesses the whole manifestation.

After deep sleep, as soon as the consciousness dawns on you of "I Am"—that is the witness. Before that moment you did not know that you are; there was no witness, no knowledge of "I Am."

You got the evidence that you are as soon as the consciousness appeared on you, but as soon as the evidence was received, that consciousness took hold of the body. As soon as that "I Am" caught hold of the body he had to behave through whatever thoughts were appearing in this manifestation. We call it disposition, or mind.

Q: Is "I Am"—the primary concept—what is actually doing the witnessing, or is that witnessing an aspect, like impersonal witnessing?

M: Consciousness is to me or to you an individual body. I say that I am conscious, you say that you are conscious; so apart from consciousness there is a principle which is aware of that consciousness.

Q: So it is the original state which is the witness of the consciousness, but that is not a personal thing. In the original condition Maharaj says that witnessing requires no effort; it automatically happens.

M: Whatever is, is the consciousness; that is all the capital we have. Once this consciousness is made clean of anything, you automatically reach the original state; but if you want to know what that state is, all this knowledge will be there. Because to know what your original state is you must understand, and you must give up this Self identification with the body and be convinced that you have no form or name. That is all that is to be done.

So long as you identify with the body-mind you are conditioned. Once you stabilize in the knowledge "I Am" unconditionally, you are the manifest "I Amness"—no more an individual. In the manifest state of "I Amness" there is no question of your doing, because you are no more an individual. Whatever happens, happens in your consciousness.

Whatever happens through this, you also know it will happen, but there is no question of doing or being anything.

Out of the rainwater good and bad things grow; no sin is attributed to the rainwater for the growth of bad things and no merit for the growth of good things. Where is the question of rebirth for the rainwater and where is the sin or merit for the rainwater?

Q: The "I" and the "I Am" without words are not the I that we think of?

M: Prior to naming it, you know you are. At that stage everything is your Self, including the dirt and the sun and the moon. That is the Self. All are your manifestation, but you are still beyond that.

One step higher now. Consciousness means this world, this manifestation, "I Amness," beingness. This consciousness has all color; it is ample, plenteous, infinite. I, the Absolute, am not the earth, the fire, the water, the air, nor the space. I am unblemished, untouched by anything. But if we consider "I" as "I Amness"—the beingness—then all this manifestation is myself, and in this manifest "I Amness" I also am untouched by any sin or merit.

Q: I would like to know why conception is more important than any other moment for determining the future.

M: Conception is the time when, unknowingly, spontaneously, the photograph of the parents is taken, besides the world situation at the moment.

Q: Tibetan Buddhism holds that it's not until maybe the third or fourth month that the soul enters the womb.

M: What is the womb?

Q: It is not my idea; I'm just repeating it.

M: All this manifest world is a combination of the five elements. We are in the five elements, we are a part of the five elements; all the play goes on in the five elements.

Q: When were the five elements born?

M: At that moment there was no time.

Q: You can't win!

M: Don't try.

Q: Who conceived the five elements, whether in time or out?

M: That primary concept, Mula-Maya, the source of illusion. Who conceived all these houses and buildings? The mental concept.

October 5, 1979

Questioner: Does the quality of your relationship with another person depend only on you or on both persons?

Maharaj: It depends on both. It is entirely the identity with the body that makes you feel there are two.

Q: Do the flowers have relationships?

M: They also have the essence of the five elements in them, and that knowledge of beingness is the essence of the five elements. If you water them they are pleased and they bloom, but if you don't water them they are displeased and angry; but we can speak while they don't have the power of speech.

Q: I'd like to know the meaning of language. Why do we talk and the flowers do not?

M: You will not know even if they are talking among themselves.

Q: What is the meaning of our language then?

M: Our words create chaos, but whatever meaning they have is only momentary; it has no lasting meaning.

Q: Small children don't speak.

M: That's why their behavior is better than yours.

Q: The kind of relationship we have with children is very different from what we have with grown-up people.

M: Because children are so innocent. You can take anybody's child and fondle it.

Q: It's a pity that first they have to learn to talk and later learn not to talk.

M: Learning to talk is done for the child's well-being. You shape the child as something is shaped from gold. Sometimes the labor charges for molding a piece of gold are more than the value of the product.

Q: I would like to know about artists. How does it happen that some person creates?

M: It is the quality of that great knowledge "I Am" that creates.

Q: Can you be an artist if you are not free from the body-mind concept?

M: It is an aid to the artist that we are in the body. The body is the support of that beingness. The moment that beingness was planted the formation of this body was taking place. The world is created for it. In the womb that knowingness is ignorant of its existence; the "I Am" is not present but the "I Am" principle is started there. All things happen unknowingly, but even to understand that is very difficult; it is beyond our comprehension.

Q: Does one become nothing?

M: In your nothingness you are perfect, you are total, and in your knowingness you are imperfect.

Q: One should give up one's self-importance then?

M: Just understand that there is no self-importance at all; realize that you have done nothing all along.

When you identify with the body-mind you become separate, you are not one with anybody. When you are the "I Amness" you are everything. To help you to understand various concepts are given, like Prakriti and Purusa, but actually there is nothing. Even such concepts form a trap. The first trap is the love to be.

Q: Is the eternal of the Absolute the eternal of the relative?

M: The Absolute is permanent, illusion is impermanent.

Q: Has it ever been pure Absolute without the impermanent change?

M: The Absolute is always. When we talk about the co-existence of the Absolute and Maya there is no question of time. The Absolute is not time-bound; beyond illusion there is no such thing as time. You cannot think whether the Absolute was without illusion because time does not exist there at all. It is not even one hundred thousandth of a second that this illusion is born, while scientists talk of this world's billions of years.

Q: When I think of the Absolute as the ocean, the waves are not the ocean, but they are still there. That's why the question came up.

M: You are not to study objectivity, the ocean and this body, the illusion. You have to understand for yourself. If you have dived deep into the sea, where are the waves? When you come out of the ocean the waves appear.

When you have no feeling of happiness or misery and no feeling of "I Amness" you are in the state of Nirguna. Recede back, prior to the thoughts.

October 6, 1979

Questioner: How do you know which is the first film?

Maharaj: The first film is when that knowingness appears on you. In that knowledge "I Am" all is contained.

Q: But what I meant is, that you are born and then you die. I want to know if we now have the memory of that?

M: According to your own knowledge is this knowingness which appeared on you the first or some other number?

Q: For me it is the first.

M: That is all you have to take for granted. Just throw out whatever you have heard or read. Tell me only what is from your own experience.

There was a person who said that he had known me for the last eleven births. I told him, "This is your concept. I do not know you." I have no faith in anything unless I have experienced it myself.

Q: There is violence everywhere, wars, and all kinds of

horrors. You long to be separate from it and at the same time you are one with it.

M: Nobody has been able to change that Maya. Just observe, without accepting or rejecting. The solution can only be when you abide in your Self. Investigate how you happened to be.

Q: Because I was created by my parents.

M: Only in that film when the film started knowing itself, "I Am"; then you came to know all this. Did you know anything before?

Q: There was nothing.

M: Exactly. That you have to understand. Direct your questioning to "Who am I?" and "What am I?"

A man was in the habit of drinking tea every morning at five o'clock; unfortunately, the principle left the body at three. Will that dead body demand tea at five o'clock? You don't touch areas which you should ponder, but you want to know all about other areas that are just a passing phase.

Q: Should we not change in order to get this knowledge?

M: You are not the one who changes. What changes is your mind, your intellect, and your body. When you come here and listen, you will be inspired to think within; later on your nature changes. Hearing is most important, and by hearing these wise words gradually the mind will change.

That knowledge "I Am" is born out of love, but the illusion has taken such hold of it that love for the "I Amness" has gone into the background. To stay with it has become increasingly difficult. Without the manifestation the love was total.

Q: Is the "I Am" identical with consciousness?

M: Yes, but that "I Amness" will be present only so long as the fuel lasts.

Q: The fuel ultimately must be love.

M: Yes. That love is all-pervading. These flowers are an expression of my love. The blooming of flowers is not an individual's expression of love, but a universal expression of love.

Q: How did the movement start?

M: There is no reason, no cause, no purpose. It is spontaneously happening.

Q: Is Maya from the point of the first movement or from the point where form is created?

M: Everything is contained in the consciousness, the whole show.

Q: Even the appearance of the illusion itself?

M: Yes, everything is illusion. Your conviction that you are born is an illusion.

Q: Who is the victim of the illusion and who will be free of it?

M: The knowledge that you are is the victim, and that is going to be liberated. A farmer sows the seeds and gets the produce. He creates and he consumes; illusion or Maya or Brahma are all your names. Who is liberated and who is bound? You only.

October 9, 1979

Questioner: When I sit in meditation there is very little thought activity, just an awareness, a very calm state of mind. Is this state something to do with going toward "I Amness" or is it just another state in consciousness?

Maharaj: That calmness is when your beingness is resting. As you have come to India but have not forgotten that you are an Australian, so likewise you should not forget what you are. Are you convinced in that fashion?

Q: Intellectually, yes.

M: Don't talk of the intellect. Are you convinced? You know that you are not the body, not the mind, and not the name given to you by someone else. You are consciousness and it has no form. You are a man because you identify with the body. If you do not identify with the body, what sex are you? After leaving the body, the vital breath and the "I Am" merge into the substratum. Then where is a man or a woman?

Q: Should one meditate on this?

M: Meditation is very necessary. During meditation you must hold on to this concept that I am not the body mind, I am the Self-effulgent knowledge only.

Q: What is samadhi?

M: Satisfaction. When you obtain your objective you feel satisfied. You want to attain a profit and when you do you feel satisfied.

Q: Samadhi is of no help in understanding the Self.

M: The state of satisfaction in samadhi is the Self. When you did not have the body, complete satisfaction existed.

Q: Is the satisfaction of samadhi total satisfaction?

M: It is an objective satisfaction that the food essence quality is there. That knowingness, which is a quality of the food essence, subsided into satisfaction.

All the Sages say to worship your own Self, but the people do not understand; they worship Rama or Krishna, etc., but in the process of worshiping all these Gods your Self sprouts.

Having listened to the talk of the Sages, the person will start focusing on the Self. He can carry on all his normal duties, but his attention will be directed to the Self; he will not be involved in anything. In this process, gradually he will attain the Highest, the Absolute. Take full advantage of a Jnani, a Guru, or a Sage that you meet, but understand what you are. Stabilize in the Self.

Because of our ignorance, all along we have depended on the mind; mind was our Guru, mind was directing and guiding us. Now I have understood that mind is not me, mind is apart from me; in this process I am apart from the body-mind. If tomorrow my body should quit, nothing will happen to me.

Q: What should one's attitude be when listening to the Guru?

M: One should be very receptive, loving, and humble and surrender completely to the Guru.

Q: How long should one stay with the Guru?

M: You have to stay with your Self, Self is the Guru. The faith in the words of the Guru should be a living faith; thoughts may come and go, but the faith should not be disturbed. You should abide in the "I Amness"; when you do that you are one with the Manifest Guru. Sat Guru is the one who watches the appearance and disappearance of this Guru "I Amness." When we abide in the Absolute that is Sat Guru. Initially you do require a person who is a Sat Guru. Those who have the urge to know the Truth will necessarily come across such a Sat Guru.

In my original true state I have no form and no thoughts. I didn't know I was, but suddenly another state appeared in which I had a form and thought, "I Am." How did this appear? The one who explains how these appearances have come about is the Sat Guru.

October 13, 1979

Maharaj: Do not be bound by imagination or ideas, keep aloof from them, let everything happen according to its own nature. Just as you are bound now by the body-mind sense, you are also bound by the relationships in this objective world, and that binding is very serious indeed. The true perspective of the Self within is the freedom that is yours.

The Self that is within is all the emptiness of the sky. Through the consciousness which has appeared on you, you view this objective world. With the knowledge that you are awake you find that the world is filled with all the objective pictures which are within you. In deep sleep there are no pictures, no objective sights at all. There is no cause for the creation of this objective world—it has come spontaneously; there was no action on anyone's part. That consciousness itself will tell the one aware of it that it is all you see.

It is very difficult to understand this; the one who has realized that the consciousness is being witnessed by the universal consciousness has reached the Ultimate. But the majority of people are wrapped up in the manifested knowledge that "I Am."

The world is within me, I am not within the world. Bhagavan [God] is the light which is the manifest world. I have realized that light, but I am not bound by it, I am not in it.

That is the state from which the manifestation is observed. Iswara [God] state is the borderline, the beginning of Nirguna—from being to no-being—of entering the Absolute field from where witnessing of this manifestation occurs. That is the beginning of the Absolute. It is not "I Amness." The Absolute cannot talk, but this talk relates to that only.

I have no method to pursue this Truth; at the most I will tell you to purify your vital breath. You will be asked to follow a meditation on nama-mantra, that's all; all other things are spontaneous.

What is the meaning of the recitation of the nama? It is the primordial music; sing this melody of name-mantra. In the process one loses one's Self and all the mischievous thoughts disappear.

Questioner: Since this manifestation is myself can I bring about certain improvements in it?

M: When you cling to the body-mind you become separate from the manifest world and you see different entities. In that state you will have all kinds of desires to improve yourself or somebody else. The next state is "I Amness", in which every action is myself, every manifest thing is myself. In that state there is no question of improving; you are just manifestation, "I am everything." Next is the Unborn state, where there is no beingness to understand "I Am." That is the highest state.

The moment I start calling myself a sanyasi [monk], I start conditioning myself: "I must have matted hair," "I must beg for food," "I must not eat this," etc. So I have not taken any pose. When food is served, whatever this body relishes I eat, whatever it doesn't I leave. Not that this is good and this is bad—nothing of the sort. Your first step is beingness: embrace the knowledge "I Am," be that. I am trying to speak of my most intimate secrets. Just as the dream world, uncalled for, has appeared and you observe it, similarly this world, uncalled for, has appeared and you are compelled to observe it. Just observe.

Spontaneously, unknowingly, your beingness has appeared. Knowingly you don't know "Now I am going to be"; only after the formation of "I Amness" do you know "I Am."

Q: Can I carry out my normal household duties?

M: Carry them out with all enthusiasm, but understand what I have told you. If you really understand this, remember it and ponder it; no special meditation is needed.

The vital breath is the cause of the mind flow; it is occupied continuously, except during sleep. Ostensibly we might be performing a ritual, reciting hymns loudly, thinking that we are performing some spiritual action, but the mind is not concentrated on that hymn, etc.; it is thinking of something else.

Q: When someone is totally enjoying what he is doing there is no sense of "I."

M: The beingness is fully absorbed in that mind inclination, but that no-being state only witnesses it.

Meditate on that principle by which you know you are and the world is. That is the very source of this manifest world. All actions are carried out by the vital breath; the language of the vital breath is called the mind. The recitation of mantra or Japa is carried out by vital breath, and this beingness is a mere witness of the actions of the vital breath. The message "I Am" is just a witness—the vital breath stimulates all activities. The support of these two entities is the food body, the food essence. The knowledge "I Am" is the film, the destiny. Finally, what is our destiny? It is that birth chemical, that film in which everything is recorded and everything is happening. Where are "you" in this? "I Amness" is a chemical in which everything that is going to happen is recorded. When this is realized you will understand that you are not an individual.

October 14, 1979

Maharaj: Have you people been moving about India together?

Questioner: Yes. Some of us have been studying Hatha Yoga, and we have also been to Sri Ramanasram for meditation.

M: Moving in pairs or in groups is for entertainment. The real quest is solitary. If you want to master Hatha Yoga you must go someplace else. For meditation go back to Ramanasram; it is a nice place. Here we have Jnana Yoga, not Hatha Yoga.

Q: But does it not help to learn to control the mind?

M: It is only when the Atman is present that there is mind. Maya is the language of the Atman.

Q: Is the Atman the thinker?

M: Atman is the observer; the mind and the prana are only activators.

Q: They do become one?

M: Because you consider yourself to be a body, you think them to be separate.

Q: What about karmic knowledge?

M: All the energy that you have is karma, but it is not the Atman.

Q: Man is always an incarnation of something he doesn't know.

M: It's only the food body. It is only because of the mind and body consciousness that these concepts come up.

Q: Are mind and the Self different?

M: They are one.

Q: What is death?

M: Only the fear of death is present, but not actual experience of death. Just as you do not have the experience of birth, you do not have the experience of death—only the fear of death.

Q: What is the experience of death?

M: It is rest.

Q: Do we have the experience of dying?

M: Not of death. At the most you may see a dead body lying there, and you are watching here.

Q: When I try to find out who I am I cannot stay long without other thoughts intruding.

M: Who knows the thoughts?

Q: I do.

M: Since you know the thoughts, you are not the thoughts. If the principle was not present who could have the thoughts?

Q: Can one be free from thought but have insight at the same time?

M: Who wants to be free from thought and have insight into something else? Who is this "I"? You are prior to the thought, you have to go back to the source.

When you ponder these talks it could be called meditation, but in actual meditation you should meditate on the meditator, contemplate the contemplator. When you do so you will know who you are. You will realize it without consulting anybody. In worldly life, as well as in spiritual pursuit, you always want to consult somebody.

Q: In our normal worldly daily life is it possible that our "I Amness" could merge in the Absolute?

M: It is not possible. That is why all these great incarnations have taken Maha-samadhi. Maha-samadhi means the beingness was merged into the Absolute.

Q: By doing Hatha Yoga I can concentrate much better, my body feels lighter. I feel that it is good for me, that I need to do it.

M: Until you know your Self you will not know what you need or do not need. Whatever you do until that moment when you know your Self is useless. You know that the body is going to be left; who is going to leave that body? Think of that.

Q: Does it mean that this identification is an obstacle?

M: Yes. It is only the concept that is the obstacle.

Q: How did we get this concept?

M: The child gets his first instructions from the mother, beginning with "We are the parents," "You are the son," "This is how you should behave," etc. Until then his needs were only physical and he did not know anything about himself. Later on he gets instructions from his teachers in school, others in his family, etc. Whatever he comes to know is what he has been told by others. The individual accepts and discusses various concepts with others, but hardly anyone gives any thought to that principle which is always present, which recognizes all this.

This knowledge is the earliest, the base of all the concepts. Knowledge is merely a name given to it—it has no name and no form. That is the source of all perception. It has no need of peace and quietude because it is itself peace and quietude. In this principle of basic quietude, without duality, no change occurs at any time. This basic principle is beyond any state. Whatever one perceives through the senses can only be a movement in consciousness, which is present when the states of waking and sleep are present. Whatever transpires in these states can only be temporary.

Consciousness is itself God, and that beingness, or consciousness, is the only thing by which is divulged to one the secret of all manifestation, all creation. Nothing else will so divulge; all else is a concept.

Until this basic principle—this basic knowledge of beingness or consciousness—divulges its own secret to you and you are intimate with it, whatever knowledge you have can only be based on concepts and is untrue; and even this basic principle, which is the source of all knowledge, is time-bound. This consciousness not only brings to you the knowledge of your own existence, but also the knowledge of the world; and when this knowledge disappears with the disappearance of the body, there is no knowledge of oneself or the world.

The secret knowledge of how "I" came into being, without any effort, will be divulged only by this conscious-beingness. Any Guru who gives you spiritual knowledge can base that knowledge only on his own concept, which he considers as Truth. The concept may be excellent; still it is a concept, and whatever you try to understand through it is not going to be permanent.

It is amazing that I am expounding this knowledge through this seed. Great Yogis and Munis who are doing penance are not able to receive it, because they are holding on to certain ideas, hoping to acquire something very great. Although ostensibly they are doing penance for the sake of Self-realization, in the process they are very happy with what they acquire, and they stabilize there.

Q: Now I have understood what you have said and I am going to study this. . . .

M: What do you mean by study? That means you are only trying to remember the concepts. What I am saying is that you must become concept-free. Put the ax to the concepts, including the concept "I Am."

Q: Are there any efforts required to eliminate the concepts so that we can know the Truth, or does it happen by itself?

M: It is spontaneous. The very concept that "I woke up" is the root of illusion.

Q: So there is to be no effort, just accept it as it is?

M: One in a million will accept this. Others want to gain something.

Q: How do we get out of the mind flow?

M: These mind things are flowing in me also, out of the vital breath, but I don't accept them. The moment an ignorant person receives an impression, he puts it to the credit of his account, he registers it in his diary.

October 21, 1979

Maharaj: This knowledge "I Am" has appeared out of love, and that love comes out in existence. When this knowledge has dawned on the Self it is absolutely happy, but after the child is two or three years old, gradually he gets involved in "I" and "mine," and he gradually loses hold of the joy that "I Am." The result of all this involvement is that he comes to the conclusion that he was born and is going to die.

This knowledge has appeared to you and you are charged with many sins and births. The accused is standing in the dock and has been sentenced to twenty-five years of rigorous imprisonment, and death by hanging at the twenty-sixth year. And he is pleading guilty! Examine yourself thoroughly: are you a body-mind? were you born? who are you? what are you? Find out for yourself. Before you were born there was nothing, there was no idea that you were taking a form; this form came to your knowledge only after your mother introduced you to yourself. After passing this examination the result will be that no idea of death will appear to you.

Questioner: What is this knowledge, knowingness?

M: This knowledge is the essence of the food that has been assimilated by the body. It is as material as the body and it will disappear, even as this fire will be extinguished. If we want to live during the next month is it not necessary that we feed our body? Suppose you have some stale food; if you put it aside it will become sour and in due course worms and insects will form therein. Is it not the food which is giving life to those worms and insects? What does it indicate? The life force which is expressed in that insect is the food essence only. The life-giving force is in this food essence, and the food essence is itself its own food.

Q: So far—if it were to hang in the air right here and not get any farther—what Maharaj said gave the impression that something like a magnetic field involved with food organizes into an "I Am." In other words, he has set up a reality of food which contains in it a field that constitutes an "I Am." I don't think that is what he is trying to get across, but it sounds like that.

M: What is that body? Out of the elements, the earth, and vegetation a body is formed—is it not so?

Q: Yes.

M: Out of that where are you?

Q: I don't know where I am.

M: Take a grain of sugar; the sugar is the essence of the sugarcane; it is sweetness only. You taste the sweetness of the sugar—you are not the sugar. What happens to that sweetness? Does it have a form?

Q: There's always the possibility.

M: When the taste has disappeared has it gone to heaven or hell? It did not go anywhere; it has merged into you.

Q: Earlier Maharaj spoke of the "I Amness" arising from the five elements. Do not the five elements also arise from the "I Am"?

M: Yes, it is a vicious circle. Understand it and get out of it. If the food body is not present, you will be whatever you were before when the food body is exhausted. Consciousness, the world, and this manifestation is an expression that "you are."

The sum total is: understand all this and do not try to interfere. All the prophets and social workers have come and gone; they could not change what is. This is the play of Maya. All this has happened out of nothingness, and it is going to the same state.

This "I Amness" is a product of the five elements and the "I Amness" again creates the five elements. So how are we to destroy that?

Q: You can't destroy it—you just have to go beyond it.

M: "I Amness" is part of the play. You are prior to the "I Amness."

October 22, 1979

Maharaj: Who has made all the wonderful mechanical and technical inventions in this world today? The child has the potentiality of all this knowledge contained within his heart, and whatever material he wanted has been provided by the five elements, but what he has created from it is as you see in the world today. That ignorance which has come out of the mother's womb gives birth to so much knowledge.

Where did Arjuna see that great universal form which Sri Krishna showed him? He saw it in that atomic consciousness in his heart. Whoever acted as Krishna and Arjuna, you are.

Questioner: I like that.

M: Are you prepared to take delivery of this statement?

Q: Yes.

M: There is no separate God to propitiate and get things done according to our will. Without doing anything you have the knowledge "I Am." Immense courage, heroism, and conviction that you are—that is Iswara, that is you. I am giving you instructions regarding your beginningless being but you prefer to be in that monkey form. You are not prepared to leave that form.

What is your object, what is your purpose? Your purpose is to retain your individuality, your personality, and to get all your needs satisfied.

This one here is coming to me so that she and all her family will have good health; that is her whole object, not Self knowledge. The family will get this minor result, but this most important result, this Ultimate, they will not get.

In this world there are no beings that are born, or living, or dead. Nothing of the sort; it is just a play in consciousness.

Q: When people believe in God what happens after death?

M: They have a peaceful death. They see God coming and then they just vanish.

Q: What about concepts of heaven and hell?

M: Whatever concept one has will happen.

Q: How can the concepts survive without the food body?

M: That "I Amness" is not extinguished immediately; it is prolonged for some time in the form of subtle body. The physical shape is gone, but the desires contained in the subtle body are not dissolved. The consciousness endures so long as a particle of the food essence persists. Sri Krishna said, "I have put these various beings on the top of a machine of this illusion; they are mechanically going round." The mechanical motive force for the movement of all these beings is Maya, "I Am," "I love."

The nature of this love is greed, great liking, intense desire to be. How passionately fond of life we are. That is the primordial Maya—"I love to be."

It is the greatest of wonders that this principle has taken such a shape, but you are enjoying it and looking at it as "I" and limiting it to the body. Now we have to find out who is the principle which has taken this form.

November 11, 1979

Questioner: People come to me and ask questions about Maharaj's teachings. How should I answer?

Maharaj: If you know the answer by all means give it, but don't consider yourself as someone superior. Should the person be only superficially interested, given an offhand answer. If there is real intent to understand—if the person is very concerned to know—discuss the question with him. Should you give correct knowledge to someone not really interested from the heart, it will damage him and others to whom he may talk.

Q: I don't know that I can explain the Self.

M: We perceive things but we must understand that we are that principle which makes perception possible. Normally an individual identifies himself with whatever he sees or perceives. You must understand the root cause of your being here. One's birth is basically associated with the womb, and that whole process must be clearly understood.

Many who call themselves Gurus have not really understood this. They go by the tradition of words. They hear something and from there they proceed, but they do not go back to the root of the matter. There have been a number of prophets, who have devised various religions according to their own ideas and concepts. These religions prescribe various codes of conduct: "Do this," "Don't do that." With all these do's and don'ts, is there any change in the basic instincts of people?

A Hindu throws a stone at a cow and the cow dies. Because of his religion, the Hindu thinks that he has committed a great sin. At the same time people of other religions slaughter a cow and eat the meat. To them there is no sin. The butcher and his family are quite happy, and well off too! They are not affected by sin. The Hindu will perform conventional acts to expiate his sin. Don't go into these different conventional codes. Go to the root.

Out of the womb of conception, out of the seed you are born. At the time of conception your beingness is in a latent condition and because of its presence the formation of the body is taking place in the fetus. Are you that?

You are not very steady mentally. Whenever I talk I want you to go to the source; instead you go forward. You don't perceive the source. Can you ask questions?

Q: How was the first body made?

M: Whether the first or the last, the process is identical.

Q: If there is no beginning it means there is nothing. Nothing began, nothing ends.

M: Here you will not get the reply of words. Dwell in the source. Stabilize there and you will get the reply.

Prakriti and Purusa, these two principles: Purusa means stationary, Prakriti is the movement. They have no body or form. We start right from space, space is steady and there is the movement of the air, Prakriti. So the Prakriti projections begin there. With the air and the sky there is friction, and out of the friction there is heat, and when this heat subsides it oozes in the form of water. The water falls as rain; where it settles the earth formation takes place, and out of the earth the sprouting of the vegetation occurs.

It is all the play of Prakriti and Purusa. When it comes to the stage of the earth and vegetation, only the formation of bodies, forms, shapes, takes place. Then various insects, animals, human beings are born. But all the formation is already decided in the space. The fate is already sealed in the space.

There is the contact of Purusa and Prakriti in the space, and its final culmination is the creation of human bodies, animals, etc. There are eighty-four million species, according to Hindu mythology.

Q: What makes the creation take place?

M: It is not real, but in the realm of Maya it is real. Understand all this game and get out of it.

Q: If it is not real why do we have to understand it?

M: So you will understand how futile it is to have this shape. In the process of inquiry you will find you are not any of that. One will be immediately liberated when one realizes, "I have nothing to do with the affairs of Prakriti and Purusa."

Q: How can that life principle in the womb be "I" or my beingness?

M: Your inquiry starts from the grosser state; that's why this "I" and "mine" question arises. Understand the whole process. In this universal process are you really one of those illusions?

Q: How do we get out of the cycle?

M: Are we not separate? You are there and I am here. Understand that this is the universal play of Prakriti and Purusa; you are not that, and you are not in that. It is simple logic. Suppose a relative of yours dies and his body is cremated. Is the relative cremated? The dead body is cremated. He is not the body. The vital breath also left the body. He is not the vital breath.

Suppose there has been an accident and hundreds of people are dead. You have heard that your dearest friend was involved, so you go to the scene and inquire. When you learn that your friend was not there, immediately you are happy and free from anxiety. Similarly, when you investigate this whole process you will find that you are not in it. Then you are free from the cycle.

Q: There are so many attractions of the world and God.

M: Why do you worry about the attractions of the world? Only when you are there the world and God are there.

Finally what we must find out is what this beingness is due to. Once you understand that beingness is the product of the food essence, you know that you can't be that beingness. There is no object for meditation. Once one comes to the conclusion that there is nothing else except one's Self, whom should he worship? That One is everything.

Q: Only One is there, but it is ample, many.

M: You know it very well but you have turned your back on it. Once one becomes a Jnani he is one with the Absolute, but as far as the body is concerned—what happens to it and its behavior—everything will be different from that of another Jnani. There is no design for a Jnani; he is not an individual. He is not concerned with how that body will act.

Q: What is the true prostration before a Jnani?

M: You may think I am a Jnani, but from my point of view, whatever I see is just child's play. The whole thing. The existence of the world and the knowledge of the world is child's play. This child is eighty-three years old and this is the play of that child's illusion.

What is the game that is being played? The infant has been born and the age belongs to that infant, not to me. Only one in a hundred thousand will really understand the knowledge which is given. Most won't give up their body sense.

All these talks are like the play between a mother and child; just entertaining, but there is no real meaning to it. The child just lives in the present, for that moment; it has no anxiety and no responsibility. The same thing happens, even if he is eighty-three years old.

This consciousness which makes perception possible is the Atma. That which is aware of the consciousness is the Brahman. I speak every day on the same subject; the trouble is that when you hear something you forget it.

November 16, 1979

Maharaj: From birth what has made the body grow? It is no power in the world; it is the power of beingness, the atom, the Self, the consciousness, call it what you will.

Various religions have given various ways of trying to please God, but the original pure form of worship is the worship of the Self.

Rulers and kings used to fall at the feet of people who in appearance were very ordinary. What is it that such seemingly ordinary people had that impelled powerful rulers to fall at their feet? This knowledge of the Self.

Many people earn a lot of money and attain worldly power, and then use them so that ultimately they lose both and live in poverty. Others, like beggars, offer their prayers for something that is only temporary, and they remain beggars.

Every person has the strength of the Self, but what happens? All that power is employed for useless things in life. That power is not retained and used for the knowledge of the Self. If this power of the Self is conserved and enlarged in obtaining the knowledge of the Self, the whole world is at your feet. Here is the advice given by the Sage Vashista to King Ramachandra: "This Self gets pleased by the strength of meditation and enjoys extreme happiness because in the ultimate happiness all other pleasures get absorbed. Even those who have not completely realized the Self, even they enjoy moments of extreme ecstasy by meditation."

Q: In what way do we waste that power?

M: You waste it in worldly affairs, in embracing each other, in gossip. Even here you sit in meditation and get a certain amount of potential power, and all that is wasted. So what is the use of doing all this? That is to be conserved and not wasted in various worldly pleasures.

Hundreds of people go to Ananda Mai, and she feeds them all sumptuously. Where does she obtain the power to get all that money? It is that Ananda Mai herself has such power that people go to her and donate money. What does Ananda Mai herself do? Nothing. She only sits there in her own happiness.

Will you keep this in mind? This is the power of Jnana Yoga; otherwise one person is like any other person. It is the power of the Self which distinguishes one from another.

Q: My energy goes up and down, up and down, in meditation. I don't have any control of it.

M: You will develop the power to control that energy in due course.

Q: I have never believed that I should force meditation. If I force it I become very dejected and tired. When it's not there of itself I can't meditate.

M: If you are not able to meditate, recite nama. If you can't meditate, recite the sacred words continuously. There was a dacoit named Vali who committed many murders and piled up a lot of sins, seven earthen pots of blood, so sinful was he. He met the Sage Narada, who told him to recite the name of Rama. Rama was not yet born. So Vali started reciting the name continuously, and because he recited it, the Absolute incarnated in the form of Rama, for the sake of Vali. So that is the power of recitation. By the power of recitation Vali exterminated all his sins and acquired many merits; because of the power of the merits Rama was born. None of us is such a sinner as Vali was. The highest worship is the worship of the Self. You are gaining a lot of merit by your meditation, but you dissipate it in worldly affairs.

Q: It is very noisy in my room, and I find my mind is noisy as well. Is it enough to come here and meditate?

M: Anywhere you like, whenever you get the opportunity to meditate, do it. You need not come here. By your deep meditation the Self is pleased and you need not go anywhere else to acquire knowledge. Your own Self will give the knowledge. The point of my talking is only this: you should know the Self, stabilize in the Self.

Q: But what is this knowing, is it a perception?

M: Start meditation and the Self will direct you. The Self is the immanent manifest spirit; don't give it a form, don't condition it in the body form. Once the Self gives up the body, what is the significance of the body? It will start decaying and decompose.

Q: When one is in meditation and there are no thoughts, can one say that the mind is dissolved in the Self?

M: Yes. What the condition of the Self is without the body will be revealed to you in meditation. The identity of the Self, or that blissfully happy state of the Self, in the absence of the body, should be revealed to you when you have the body. In spite of the body you have to reach that state.

Q: When I meditate and the mind is focused, but not on anything, there seems to be a borderline state between "I-ness" and the Self. You can watch thoughts happen; then sometimes you have a feeling there is some presence, as if someone has come into the room, even though you don't see him. That kind of feeling.

M: You might feel that but your attention should be on the Self, the meditator.

Q: But your mind is not focused on the feeling; it comes without warning.

M: In the process you will acquire much knowledge also, but your attention, your interest, must be the Self, not whatever you get. The Self will become manifest, infinite, boundless. Presently that which is now conditioned in a personality will be broken up and it will become manifest, unbounded.

Q: When I am in the thought-free state I have this feeling of total balance, no happiness, no misery, just balance. Is this correct?

M: Yes; the state of the Self, no pleasure, no misery. This

is called identity with the Highest, when you don't know that you are. So long as the vital breath is present mind will be also; be in the Self, don't get involved with the vital breath and the mind. Ignore the mind.

November 17, 1979

Questioner: I am told that I am the manifest, immanent Spirit. How is it that I get involved in this body?

Maharaj: If you are the immanent Spirit, what is that other you that is involved in this body state? Is it some other thing? Body, immanent Spirit, and you. It is nothing else but the dynamic, immanent Spirit. Its manifestation occurs in the form of the guna "I Am," it understands itself as "I Am." Then this guna involves itself in the activities in the world through the three gunas. That is the quality.

Q: Who am I?

M: Whatever name you want to give yourself, give it! You may name it Brahma, or Iswara, or anything you like. The names are only necessary for your worldly activities, or for communication.

If the accusation that you are born is accepted as correct, then you are an embodied personality, the world is correct, is real; so also this manifest Brahma is correct. But when you start investigating your own Self you come to the conclusion that birth is not a fact, it is unreal.

So if this birth is not a fact, this beingness also cannot be a fact, because beingness has appeared. Beingness means also this manifest world, so the manifest world is not real. Therefore, investigate the Self.

Presently this level of knowledge and your level of understanding—do they tally? You!

Q: Yes.

M: I have been told that I was born, I have not directly

experienced being born. This is indirect knowledge. Un-knowingly this beingness has appeared; suddenly I know "I Am," and this knowledge is direct. When you investigate the "I Am" do you find any link between the birth and the knowingness?

Q: No.

M: When the birth is disproved, the great noble meaning of spirituality and the meaning of this world—everything—is disproved. What is the activity coming out of this beingness?

Q: Whatever you like.

M: You have to meditate, contemplate this particular point. You cannot knock out what I say by mere words. You have to contemplate it.

Q: I am finished.

M: I agree, and I am fully convinced that you are adroit with words. People follow certain disciplines with insistence, but they don't try to investigate the root cause. If they come face to face with that root they will be stunned into silence.

I am not telling you this to run you down, but I am anxious that you should get the factual knowledge. I have great respect for you.

Q: I came for what I have.

M: Still I have to say that you have not fully understood your presence, your beingness. If you really understood it, everything would be thrown overboard.

Q: I'm not arguing. I'm not looking for approval, because I have not made any statement.

M: I have the least idea that you have come back here to seek my approval for your accomplishments.

Q: Well, if you think that, you are right.

M: "I Am" is a quality, an attribute indicating beingness, but the Self is not a quality. For that Ultimate Self no worldly knowledge is necessary. Words are not called for. But for the sustenance of this beingness, these words and worldly knowledge are necessary.

Q: Yes, I know this. At one time I wanted the knowledge, then I came to see that I was already it.

M: The beingness has appeared, and in the beingness all this play is going on. This is also unreal, but if anybody asks me what this is, I will give it a title—it is all Brahma's play; because of the beingness the play has started.

All will merge into the play of this Brahma. What is the cause of the billions of stars, the moon, and the sun? All the dirt and refuse which is lying stored on the surface of the earth turns into gas, and out of this gas the luster is appearing. The gas is formed out of the food which you consume, and when the gas is lit up the torch of the knowledge "I Am" is sustained. Is this not a gas which has finally come out of air and water? Is not the one who is talking the product of the gas due to food and water?

The flame of knowingness is sustained by the gas of the food. The knowingness is something like the taste of sweetness, without a tongue. It is the subtlest. It is subtler than space.

November 18, 1979

Maharaj: The God principle in the body is going to cast off the body. While you are living get introduced to that principle. Know that principle and be one with it. The body will not be with you always.

Consciousness is the reflection of the Awareness that is the Absolute. Consciousness will remain only as long as the body is there. Keep thinking on this point. While we are alive it is everything, and we must abide in it, but keep in mind that the consciousness is going to disappear.

The food that we eat will disappear as waste within twenty-four hours, but is the principle that is in us going to waste like the body? Do you really give a thought as to the purpose of your coming here? Are you the body? You must find out what you are. You must investigate and find out.

You must ponder this very seriously. Only then come here and listen to me. Right here and now, while you have the body with you, find out what you are.

What do you understand by spirituality? Exactly what is it that you are doing in the name of spirituality?

You consume food and drink water, and you throw it out as fecal matter and urine. In the same way you have to discard the body. Remember also, the food is very delicious when you eat it, but later on it has a stench, it becomes fecal matter.

That indwelling Spirit, that Godly immanence residing in this body—inquire about that. Some significance is given to the body because the indwelling Spirit is Godly. If the indwelling Spirit quits the body, the body becomes as fecal matter.

Why are you putting in so much effort for this body which is just going to become waste?

Whatever harmony or friendship you might enjoy with other people lasts only so long as the minds are in tune with each other. Once you disagree, the mind is in disturbance and you discard the friendship. Remember, once the vital breath leaves the body, the body is going to be disposed of. How long are you going to pamper the body?

Questioner: What is renunciation?

M: Renunciation is to understand and discard what is not useful to you. You understand what this "I Amness" is and what that principle is prior to the beingness. That is your Self. It is not the body. What I am telling you is the most important purpose of your visit here.

There was a disciple of Tiku Baba, a Muslim Sage, who used to visit me daily in my bidi shop. One day he brought a message that there was a lot of trouble in the world and asked what should be done. I told him, "Investigate the cause of the birth which has taken place. Apply the cause as a medicine to all the worries and miseries of the world. Then make bhajans in its name." After listening he started to dance. Ask the creator of the body what the antidote for the misery is. All the doctors and psychiatrists—what are they going to do? How are they going to handle the patient? Ask the creator itself. Do you put what I am saying into practice?

Q: I am trying.

M: By trying can you put that to use?

Q: By your Grace.

M: Where is the question of Grace? It is already there with you. You are it. Find out how this creation of the body has happened. Due to what? What is the cause?

In this world there are crores of statues called human bodies; each has a different face. Now you find out who made this image which you call the body. What is it made of and who is the sculptor? Is he there or is he not present in that body?

December 28, 1979

Questioner: What does a Jnani think about all the different religions in the world?

Maharaj: A Jnani does not concern himself with the various religions in the world. Those have been started by human beings. What has man created out of his various religions? Very little happiness or satisfaction and a great deal of jealousy, hatred, disturbance, and differences. Man torments himself by his concepts and imaginations about various religions. Every nation has several religions; all is the play of the five elements.

Each person has entangled himself in certain concepts of his own and is keen on perpetuating them. The unfortunate thing is that he does not see the fundamental basis of what he himself is. For one who has realized this basis there can be no fear of death.

Q: Was Hitler a product of his own thought or a product of the food essence?

M: He was a product of the five elements, so there is no sense in personalizing him. The true nature has no form. Whatever appears is a result of the five elements.

Q: How does a Jnani distinguish between a Jnani and a Hitler?

M: A Jnani does not distinguish between them at all.

Q: How did they arrive?

M: They have just come out of the five elements. Out of three or four raw materials a cook can concoct various dishes, each with a different taste, but basically they are from the identical materials. So if you ask where did this dish come from, what can you say? It is a mixture of those materials.

Q: India has millions of oppressed persons. Some want to help them, but the teacher warns us not to assume any such aim.

M: When there is a certain state of affairs, it is all movement, it keeps on changing. There must be some people who have the capacity to remedy the condition. Whatever turns up as a remedy is part of the play of the elements; so where does the individuality come in? Everything is part of the happening.

Q: How did the five elements arise? Who is responsible for them?

M: You. Find out how this body arose. The original question takes you back millions of years. Let us take a nearer one, that is, your own body. Find out how this body arose and you will come to the answer of your original question.

We have this body, mind, and consciousness. Find out how much of it is temporal, seasonal, and what is permanent, which will not change. Once you find that out there is nothing more to do.

Q: I understand, with conviction, that just as the body and the breath have appeared they are going to disappear, and this consciousness also will disappear, but there must be something which is changeless and permanent. How do I find it?

M: There is a little water in a pot and you pour it into the sea. So which part of the sea will want to know whether it is joined with the water in the pot? How do you know which part was separate? So that tiny bit of consciousness merges with the total consciousness.

Q: After the death of the body this consciousness will merge with the universal consciousness. While the body is present is it possible to know the Ultimate state?

M: When one is merged who is it that will want to know? Many people, particularly Westerners, feel that their questions have not been answered to the point. Is this view correct?

Q: No. Maharaj answers what we really need to know, and when he answers I always realize that I would be better off not asking many of my questions. He always answers what I want to know anyhow.

M: The ideal answer is to know who is striving for happiness and suffering difficulties. What is the real that I am striving for.

Q: Some sects in Christianity stress that if you really accomplish all the promises in the Bible you will disappear at death, rather than be buried. I was convinced of that for years, because when I was young I had a Guru who did disappear in front of us and reappear many miles away at the same time. I used to think that this was important. Of course, I gave that up a long time ago, but still, when I am with Maharaj, I can see it is an absolutely ridiculous idea.

M: There is no end to the miracles that can happen in the world, but they are still of the manifest. There have been many powerful minds and powerful beings, who, by their penance or strength of mind, have acquired powers and performed miracles. What has happened to them?

Q: The same thing that happens to everyone.

M: If they have had the experience of their true Self, such people would not be trying to acquire powers.

Q: Many Westerners who come here believe that if you become a Jnani or become enlightened, everything improves. This is what they seek.

M: Let them come. Each one comes with his own concepts. Whatever their concepts they will realize that ultimately there is no accounting. This consciousness is not going to remain with me—that I know—so what have I got to do with anything, any concepts or ideas that anyone tells me?

Q: Is it possible to transcend this consciousness which I have?

M: Where is the need? Have you started this consciousness? Why are you taking this ego responsibility for this consciousness? You did not ask for it.

Q: I am tremendously grateful to Maharaj. What is most different is that, regardless of anything, he answers what is most helpful and right, but people want to make the teachings into a system, which ruins them. But Maharaj doesn't worry. He just says on Wednesday that red is black and on Friday that red is white, but the answer is correct at the time, because it changes the orientation of the questioner. It is tremendously valuable and unique.

M: Like an actor who plays different roles.

January 1, 1980

Maharaj: As soon as the Unmanifest became the manifest a state of duality arose, and everything that takes place in the manifest is time-bound. You think that I am talking to you as an individual, but I talk to the manifest and not to the individual. The individual is merely a figment of the imagination.

You are a gynecologist, you deal with birth and medicine. What has given rise to the births is the five elements. When the baby is one or two years old its existence is made known to it by the mother. The mother says, "You are a girl, I am the Mother," etc. The baby merely acts until that time. Later on, whatever knowledge is obtained is what one word gives to another word. It is based on words.

When a person is operated on medicine is administered to make him unconscious, and when he comes back to consciousness and begins to feel pain, another medicine is given to make him unaware of the pain. Later on he doesn't feel hungry, so another medicine is given to stimulate the appetite. All that which gives rise to the baby is nothing but another kind of medicine, a natural medicine, made of the five elements. Whatever is, is of the five elements. If this is clear, where do you, as an individual, come in? What does one take pride in, as an individual?

Questioner: What is to be done? What is the aim in life?

M: To see one's Self as one is, to see one's true nature.

Q: How is that stage to be obtained?

M: By continuous Japa [repetition of mantra].

Q: What do you mean by Japa?

M: Japa means "take care" in Marathi. You only take care of something which you have a desire to maintain, so the Japa is based on desire.

Q: So the sadhaka is one who does the sadhana in order to achieve something?

M: It is true that the sadhaka has a desire to achieve something. These things are given to a mumukshu, the first stage, when one feels that there is something beyond this material universe. The mumukshu is still concerned with his body-mind, but when he becomes convinced that he is not the body-mind he goes to the stage of a sadhaka, where he is convinced that he is the beingness or the consciousness. Ultimately he comes to the conclusion that he is not the beingness, because the beingness depends on the food and is also time-bound.

Q: Is there any value in repeating the mantra, and, if so, to what extent?

M: Yes. By repeating the mantra with a great deal of concentration the inner receptacle in the body is purified so that one becomes receptive to such inner knowledge that may come, and the mind disappears into a spirit of reality.

What generally happens is, one starts repeating the mantra and then wonders if the tea is ready, or the telephone rings, etc.

Q: My patients will ring up and I must deal with them. So how do you get out of the obligation?

M: You must make up your mind what you want. If your desire is so keen that whether the body lasts or not you must have it—if the determination is that great—then it must come, but if you want something in the material world, it is not possible. The true pupil keeps this in mind and meditates. This beingness in the body is so powerful that you will be able to see whatever deity you meditate on. It is basically the strength of the beingness. Most people do not have time to spare to repeat the name, or whatever the sadhana is. Ultimately, the aim is to forget one's individuality.

Q: Does it mean that one shouldn't have anything to do in the world? One must give up the world?

M: The crucial question is, by whom? Whatever has brought about conception is the primordial seed of the entire universe.

Q: I have a question about Babaji. Was his ability to sustain himself for so many years learned before becoming a Jnani?

M: That ability is not acquired. It is something that happens in nature, in the manifest world. There is no law or reason; all kinds of miracles happen, anything can happen. The beingness has stuck to the body, has not merged, it still remains. In the traditional Hindu literature there are two entities who have seen any number of universes created and destroyed. As soon as the conception took place and the film was created, the future was photographed and that was their destiny. There is no reason; it just happens, one of those miracles of nature.

Q: The followers of this man Babaji say that for centuries he is supposed to have been appearing and disappearing in the Himalayas. What Maharaj is saying is that such a man must have had that ability by birth or that he learned it from somebody before he became a Jnani. After he became a Jnani he would not appropriate any powers to sustain the body.

M: I know that this beingness is time-bound, so why should I worry about somebody else? Why does anyone worry about this? Whatever has been produced will ultimately take its end and go back into the state from which it came. At the end of that happening it will go.

Q: Does one discard all the Yoga when one becomes a Jnani?

M: That by which one was able to become a Jnani will itself disappear. There is an insect whose sting causes itching and nausea. When the insect is removed the itching and nausea stop. All the itching and nausea in life is because of that tiny speck in the Brahma-randhra; because of that beingness all these troubles arise in the consciousness. Once you know that you are not that, everything is over.

The moment the Sat Guru makes everything clear, there is no need for Japa, or mantra, or anything. If you have understood what I have been telling you there is no need of any sadhana. There is no need to do anything, and you can do anything.

January 2, 1980

Questioner: In the unmanifest, in the awareness, a feeling "I Am" becomes total consciousness, but the consciousness within oneself, which is time-bound, the knower of this consciousness cannot be that consciousness. He is totally different. A Jnani is established in the state prior to all knowledge.

Maharaj: Where did you come from? Who directed you here?

Q: I am from Australia and I was here before, three years ago, for a few days.

M: Have you felt any effects from when you were here before?

Q: Yes, a change.

M: You have been coming here for knowledge, but would you be prepared to accept life without the body?

Q: Yes. What are the characteristics of life without the body?

M: That is unchanging; the life with the body is changing, transient. Your true nature is such that you are not aware of the consciousness or the waking and sleep states.

The trouble is that people do not really understand with conviction that the body, breath, and consciousness are time-bound, and the beginning and end of life is a tiny thing that has happened in the state that is permanent. At the end of the day the consciousness will disappear and no one will want to know the road by which to travel.

In life one comes with a ticket, and at the end of life one must go; there is no appeal. Realize that the beginning and end of life is a journey with a time-bound ticket, and know that at the end of the ticket whatever has come will go; and be a witness of that, step out of it.

Q: There seems to be a lot of evidence that consciousness does somehow continue after death.

M: It is a concept. Actually no one has an experience even of the birth and death of this life.

Q: How did they happen?

M: Have you had any dreams?

Q: Yes.

M: You are also present in your own dreams and you see as someone totally different; at the end of the dream it all disappears.

Q: Why did I get into this body consciousness?

M: You are sleeping safe and sound in your bed, warm and comfortable. So why do you convey yourself in your dreams to a state where you are struggling for breath and dying in a nightmare? All this manifest is only a dream of the Unmanifest and is not really happening.

That which makes us believe that we are is the cause,

and at the end of it we are back in our original state. One who knows this has no fear of anything that is happening.

Q: Would it be reasonable to say that the Jnani has certain spontaneous observable characteristics, one of which might be compassion?

M: Exactly what do you mean by the word compassion?

Q: Everyday Maharaj meets people and tries to communicate a kind of knowledge. Why does he bother?

M: This compassion is not for the individual, but that beingness which has trapped itself into identifying with a number of individuals.

Q: Is this compassion a spontaneous relationship between the Absolute and the consciousness?

M: At the very point and at the same time that the Unmanifest became manifest the reason for this compassion arose spontaneously.

Q: I understand. When the Jnani's body dies his true state is unconditioned, but this compassion doesn't die. Does the Jnani then reincarnate himself? What happens to the compassion that has originated itself and vanished?

M: The entire manifest world is a very clear expression of the spontaneous arising of this compassion. One does not realize the instant expression of this compassion in the world. Before the baby is born the milk is formed in the breast of the mother, and the compassion to feed the baby arises at the same moment. A woman is not inclined to feed someone else's baby.

Q: What I was getting at is whether after death a seed remains, a kind of continuity, whether the Jnani wishes to take a new body.

M: The very conception of something continuing from one birth to another is wrong. When you become a full Jnani you will understand that without you even the five elements will not have any life. The knowledge I am giving now is like feeding infants, but when you have the full knowledge you will understand that your beingness sustains the entire universe.

This beingness is of no value, it brings nothing but unhappiness, and it is time-bound, but simultaneously, so far as the manifest world is concerned, the tiniest being alive is the support of the entire universe.

This consciousness that one has is of a manifold nature—it can adopt any form it likes—whereas your true nature is full in itself, unchanging.

You have knowledge of the nature of man and of the nature of consciousness. What more knowledge are you seeking?

Q: Actually I am seeking to go beyond knowledge.

M: There is really no going, either beyond or prior to. That state is there. Man thinks he has to go from one state to another, but there is no going. Is there anything further you are seeking?

Q: Just to have all the false attachments, false identification fall off.

M: That is the whole trouble, one thinks that certain misconceptions have come to him. All those concepts are movements in consciousness, and once the consciousness itself disappears the movements that have come with it also disappear. You are already in that state, there is nothing to acquire. Now you know this, and, for you, all this is useless.

Q: Right. I would like Maharaj to explain about the Brahma-randhra. I am familiar with the Yoga teaching on it, but Maharaj's is slightly different.

M: There are two things, the world and one's presence, the feeling of presence, that is, the consciousness, the beingness. That is Brah-ma, "I am present"; randhra means the tiniest of apertures, and in that aperture is the silent, primordial sound, which gives you the impression that you are, but you really are not. This sound in that aperture gives you the feeling that you are, but be sure that you are not.

Q: Very good.

M: I take my stand in the original state where I was not aware that I am. This body and the beingness has come, but knowing its nature I do not expect anything from it.

When a Yogi is totally absorbed in his meditation or Yoga, this soundless sound so fills him that he becomes drunk with it for a while and then it subsides.

When the body dies this individual consciousness will

merge with the total consciousness, but even so, that total consciousness knows that it is, and so long as one knows that it is, it is in a state of duality.

January 3, 1980

Maharaj: The moment the sense of beingness arose there was a sense of duality. The manifest world is full of movement which creates and destroys innumerable forms all the time. This consciousness is of a universal nature; just like space. The consciousness within the body is a minute experience, but its nature, its quality is essentially the same, exactly like space.

The imagination and memory create a body and a personality, and the manifest assumes wrongly that it is a body and a personality.

Questioner: What causes the beingness to arise?

M: Just as you have no cause for your dream, there is no cause for the beingness. Explain to me how you have a dream. It is causeless; therefore it is without logic.

All that we see in this manifest world is exactly like a picture on the television screen.

Whom do we call parents? Only two physical forms; if they disappear we consider that our parents are gone. That which has brought about my beingness without my knowledge constitutes my parents, that is the root.

It is only because I am that I see the world and think of God; therefore God is because I am. If I am not, God is not. I will give you a formula which will do everything for you: think continuously in terms of "I am God, there is no God without me." When you are firmly established in this, whatever is unimportant will gradually fade away.

A step further: I have told you to say "I am God," but now what I am getting at is not the words "I am God," but that which was prior to the understanding of the words. That is God and that is you, not the words.

The postman comes here to deliver the mail. He may be a small man but he is fully aware that he represents the government. My feeling that I am is the registration of the presence of God.

The original question was how to go beyond this consciousness. The consciousness is time-bound, but it is the only capital we have and that is why it is so important.

Q: I haven't got the hang of it yet.

M: That is because the identity with the body is so strong; that is not easy to give up.

Q: Give us some trick by which we can give up this identity with the body.

M: The only answer is continuous practice of meditating and thinking on what I have said. Gradually this self-limitation will disappear and the sense of separation will go. For the riddle to be solved one has to meditate deeply over a long period. Meditation means the beingness absorbing itself into the beingness. Over a long period of this kind of meditation one will come to know the Knower of this beingness.

I am the Knower of this consciousness. I can only know something else, I cannot know myself; and that riddle will solve itself by continuous deep meditation.

You are now convinced, are you not, that you are the knower of the consciousness?

Q: Yes.

M: You are convinced, but there is still a mental identification with the body which makes you feel that something good is going to happen to you. Now you have a certain amount of knowledge and it makes you feel very happy. This knowledge has driven away ignorance. In the washing away of the ignorance the knowledge will also disappear, only you remain.

The sound that must be heard is the silent sound. Only the silent sound can hear the actual sound.

Q: Is God the equivalent of the manifest formless?

M: God is the soundless sound. It is in the manifest because all we are talking about is the manifest; the Unmanifest cannot talk at all.

January 5, 1980

Maharaj: People do not believe me when I tell them that they do not know themselves. You have allowed yourself to be enticed by what is not the truth; by identification with the body you have lost that knowledge.

Questioner: Who is that "you"?

M: Who is asking this question?

Q: Since this individual beingness depends on the body how can one say that the body cannot be given too much importance?

M: We give too much importance to individuality. This consciousness in the body remains only so long as the body lasts. We think that when the body is destroyed the consciousness is also destroyed. It is not destroyed; it becomes one with the universal consciousness.

This beingness, which is our most prized possession and which we want to retain at all costs, preferably for all time to come, is dependent on the body and will only last as long as the time limit for each individual existence.

The subject must be separate from the object which it perceives. The body must disappear, no matter how intensely one may wish otherwise. The Self is separate; it will merge with the Universal Being.

The Self is totally different from what the listener imagines it to be. I address the actual listener, not what the listener thinks he is. There are various kinds of knowledge in this world, but the only true knowledge is knowledge of the Self.

Q: Because of my experiences, I have had visitations and

guidance from many Saints. Maharaj says in the book that we receive help from many different persons. What are those persons who give us help?

M: They all arise in your own being, from your own consciousness. They are not separate from you.

Q: So the statement in the book was not complete?

M: That answer was to a particular person, and what I have told you now is the answer for you.

Q: I can shut it all out, or should I be receptive? It is very hard to open the door to the Guru and keep everything else out. Meditation on the Guru is very important.

M: If the guidance of those so-called sages or guides is acceptable to you, accept it; otherwise reject them and ask them to proceed. If you have a vision of a gigantic god whose head is touching the heavens, unless you are its support where is the vision? I am not telling you what you should or should not do. I want you to be your Self, the very **support of all. Your seeking advice will depend on your own level, your purpose.**

By his teachings my Guru has taken me to the state before there was any conditioning, any experience of any kind. The Yogi who gets absorbed in the silent sound is there before the silent sound. You have reached the state where these things happen, but remember, you are there before.

You are having all these wonderful meditations. If you persist in your association with me you will lose everything.

January 11, 1980

Maharaj: Before the nine months imprisonment in the womb what was my condition? I don't know, but I conclude that this imprisonment occurred because of the agreement of the male and female. The anada [bliss] which the couple enjoyed is now in the form of this particular consciousness. How can you account for this? Find out the futility of it; you can't find the truth there. You have to come to the point: "How can this be the truth—can that which depends on the body be the truth?" Use your intellect.

In order for this consciousness which you love so much to be, the body must be there.

Questioner: Would the body have any purpose for that which is before its conception?

M: What is your state?

Q: The body.

M: Is this body a form of food?

Q: Yes.

M: And in the form of food is the memory of your being, and that is the consciousness of "I love."

This knowledge is very rare. With it you can make plenty of money and get the things of this world; you can go about here and there and talk about this knowledge and people will worship you if you want.

Q: I don't want that.

M: From my angle you are nothing, you have no identity; but if you feel you have an identity you can go ahead in the world with this knowledge which I have imparted so far.

The original illusion, which is without any words, will not stop acting. You cannot remove the original illusion—it has to continue; subsequent illusions you can remove, but not the original illusion.

Q: I see.

M: This will continue. You will see grass growing, water flowing in the rivers, waves on the ocean, etc. That is the original Maya—you can't stop that, it is the very nature of the illusion. The original Maya has no color, no shape, nothing at all. You cannot conceive of that original Maya.

Can you use this for anything? You might accumulate enormous wealth. Who is going to benefit? After your death your children might use part of it, the government might take part. It is all public, all non-personal. Your knowledge will not remain personal, it is meant for others. If you understand at the time of death what you are, that you were never a person, it is enough. Don't feel that you are a personality and that you can do something for yourself. There is no person.

Whatever you earn you will try to protect, but it is not going to comfort you at all. You are not going to see the world again, so everything is to be used by others, not you. Right now, try to know what this consciousness is.

You are dependent for your living on the strength your body gets from the food you eat, and the essence of this food and food body is this consciousness "I Am." Your beingness is within you, not somewhere else.

The only thing to be understood is this: This beingness is because of the Satva guna, which behaves in the world according to the other guna [rajas and tamas]. You are not any of these. The attributes refer to everything manifest, and the expression of the Satva guna is this beingness.

January 13, 1980

Maharaj: **By our** own concepts we decide that something is dirty or not. Some people process the excrement of a wild boar as a remedy for certain diseases, and it is extremely effective, even for those on the point of death. What is otherwise considered as dirt is used as a medicine. Even the human body is created out of what might be considered as dirt. Would one give importance to one's individuality if one considered what this body is?

As far as I am concerned, I have no faith in anything which has been told, not even what has been told by the Vedas. Only my own experience.

You have had many visions. Is there any truth in the visions? What is the basis for any visions?

Questioner: The "I Am" consciousness.

M: In the traditional view Brahman is supposed to have created the world, Vishnu to maintain it, and Shiva to destroy it. Is not this Brahman who creates the world the same as the Brahma-randhra out of which the sense of "I Am" comes? Who is this Brahman other than this "I Amness"? All these names are given to it. Whatever is time-bound is created out of the beingness. Have you understood the basic concept?

Q: Whatever happens in our experience is all to be viewed as neither good nor bad?

M: Why do you even talk like this? What is the point?

Q: Right.

M: The only thing to be thought about is: "How did this form and being come about? I didn't want to have them." What is the basis on which I view any one who comes here?

Q: It is all the same thing.

M: That is "I Am"; what I am the others are. If you accept what I say, what idea do you have about yourself?

Q: The self we know is no more real than what we know of others. In other words, it is all illusory.

M: What do you think will happen to you?

Q: I hope eventually to discover the part that is real and not be limited to the time-bound.

M: Why? Having realized that what one sees is false, who is the "you" who is searching for the real? Is there any answer?

Q: No.

M: Having made this search what have you found? What is your conclusion?

Q: I have settled into just seeing what occurs.

M: Is this expectation or is it because one is compelled to?

Q: Neither one, it just is, with no expectations. That is **where I am right now. Does it mean that, other than na-**ture, there is nothing?

M: Other than the word nature there is nothing on which we can hang our support. Do you know out of what we observe the creation? How do you understand the creation of anybody in name and form?

Q: Only in terms of our own experience.

M: What is that?

Q: I start with myself, what I observe within myself. I do not build any theories behind it.

M: What are you observing?

Q: Everything that comes and goes.

M: The beingness is witnessing spontaneously. How is the witnessing of your beingness going to be useful to you?

Q: I really don't know, but I accept that there is a value in observing it as being unreal.

M: After understanding this, what is the purpose of your existence?

Q: Is the purpose of the body to get that state which is prior?

M: Who says that? Give me his identity.

Q: I can't.

M: If you can't give any identity why are you speaking?

Q: Simply in obedience to Maharaj.

M: That is because the questioning itself becomes impossible at this stage. Since the questions are not, what is the use of staying here?

Q: We don't have a complete insight into being nothing; there's a little we need to get rid of.

M: That which is totally dissolved or obliterated is observed, That which IS always is not perceptible. That principle ever remains.

Any one of you who has clearly understood what I have said today need not come here again.

Q: I have understood intellectually, but I have not realized it. I am still sick; that's why I have to come here.

M: When you are fully convinced that whatever you see is unreal why hang on to the unreal principle?

Q: We must have recourse to that faith or belief?

M: Yes. What is that faith or belief—it is only the principle "I Am."

January 14, 1980

Maharaj: I have put my ax at the very root; there is no question of any sprouting. Whatever my state was prior to the child is my true state. The moment the child appears is also the moment of your first experience of the world. Your body needs a lot of care, special foods. What is it that you are nursing? That beingness; you are trying to protect it.

Questioner: So that which is there before beingness becomes Maharaj's conscious experience?

M: Yes, that is the eternal state, while this beingness is time-bound.

Q: Maharaj knows this from experience? How does he know?

M: Because I prevail prior to anything. I ever exist. Paramatman, Parabrahman—those are the titles of my state. Prior to the appearance of childhood, that is my eternal state. In that state there was nothing, and in that state I have no knowledge of anything.

Q: That is true for everybody. Some people know it and some don't.

M: I have no association with anyone in that state. I am—always—without words.

Q: How do we acquire the consciousness?

M: When you swallow this beingness state, what remains is that state.

Q: In one of the Upanishads there is something about "I Am alone, let me be many." Did you feel lonely?

M: This sentence occurred when beingness appeared. When that vibration first appeared it was only beingness; then it felt "I am alone" and wanted to become plenty. I reject the Upanishads and all those profound teachings because they do not touch me. Whatever is written in philosophy is only ignorance. All the three gunas are full of emotion, emotion-bound, and are not the truth.

I am ever non-objective, unmanifest, I am ever in that

state. It is the Yoga Maya, that beingness, through which everything is happening. It is something like a photochemical which is expressing that image; so this beingness expresses it in the world.

Q: The experiencer is an object which is taken to be a subject; there is no experiencer.

M: Is this only theory or is it a practice?

Q: Practice. I have been looking everywhere for an "I" and I cannot find it.

M: Do you have this firm conviction always?

Q: Yes.

M: The word "I" is not there, but the manifestation is.

Q: Maharaj has said that only the false wants to continue.

M: Correct.

Q: I still feel the sense of "I."

M: The sense of "I Am" is always there; only when it identifies with the body it is called the ego.

Q: Why did I come to Maharaj? Does he know?

M: Because you wanted confirmation that whatever you say is correct. You insist that whatever you say is correct. Those who come here presume that they are knowledgeable. I understand that they don't have an iota of knowledge; therefore I tell them to sit here and listen to the talks, and spontaneously, automatically, all doubts will be cleared.

People bring all these knickknacks—the house is full of them; but I don't belong to them, I am apart. Someone brought this carpet, which cost him four thousand rupees; it is not mine, I use it. Similarly, the beingness, in the realm of beingness, is being used or experienced, but I am not it.

This knowledge of beingness has appeared, and it is going to disappear. The one that observes the appearance and disappearance of beingness sees it without eyesight, and that witness does not relate to this realm of "I Amness" or beingness.

The entire world is the body of the beingness, the play of beingness. Take the example of the TV screen on which you view various scenes. You might see rocks, trees, or an ocean, but it is all the play of light. Similarly, the manifest world is the play of beingness. On the TV screen who is playing the part of people, rocks, trees, mountains, etc.? It is the light only. Having realized this, when you go into quietude you **will understand that in the cell of beingness many universes** are playing about. Why do I have such respect for the foreigner? Because he is very serious; whatever he pursues, he proceeds to the end.

Q: Then all the archaryas are not in India?

M: They neither belong to Europe nor to India. They are the products of the play of the five elements.

I am not concerned with any miracles except the three within myself. The first is that I am able to see the world; the second is that the world is contained in that tiny spot of consciousness which I am; the third is that from that no-being state this beingness has come. Give thought to these miracles.

"Whatever is, is you." These are the words my Guru gave me. Since then all my inquiries have been directed within. Surely I, who am having the experience of this world, must have been prior to it. When I see something and say I understand it, that which I was before I acquired this form must be there to understand it. If you must give a name to it you can call it God, Iswara; names are not important. Who has given this name? I have given this name.

January 16, 1980

Maharaj: Because of this fraudulent world which is created out of spit people are sincerely ashamed. Therefore they would not like to expose or parade the very mouthpiece from which that spit was ejected. That's why they want to keep it in hiding always. Considering this aspect how can you have any ego at all? A most despicable state of affairs. You are emanating from where and proceeding to where?

Questioner: From nowhere to nowhere.

M: Would you care to stay for two weeks more?

Q: Oh, yes.

M: Your self-esteem will be fully exposed; would you like that?

Q: I have nothing to hide; only Maharaj told me to stand up and fight.

M: With the help of a telescope I observe all the manifest world.

Q: Is this Maharaj's belief or is it his experience?

M: There is no necessity for belief.

Q: Then why does Maharaj say "I," "I was," or "I am"?

M: This talk happens in the telescope.

Q: What is the state when you take away the telescope?

M: When you didn't know you were, that is your true state. Although you have imbibed knowledge, still you want to do something to further yourself. I am the Unmanifest, and with my manifestation, my form and body is all this world. I don't know how you identify yourself. You might presume that you have certain knowledge but with that you want to develop your egotistic sense only.

Q: Do you have to lose all your knowledge?

M: You have to understand; you need not reject the knowledge.

Q: From what was said earlier I understand that there is no meditation needed, but Maharaj told me to keep quiet and to meditate to realize what I am.

M: From where do you know that you are? In the knowingness everything is.

Q: I just feel it. Through the telescope I have understood that I am not the telescope.

M: You have not understood. You presume that you have, but you have not understood.

Q: I have understood the words, but I have not understood?

M: Whatever you have understood, it is something else; you do not understand your Self.

A donkey is going by on the road and you inquire about the donkey. How are you concerned with it? Here you will not be able to satisfy your itch for talking. Elsewhere you can talk and be satisfied with the talk.

Q: I feel that I have nothing to do. I will perform my meditation and everything will come through it.

M: What I mean by meditation is to reject all experience and be in the experienceless state. To understand this you have to meditate. What is the experience? The experience "to be." The one who observes this being and no-being state is the True state.

You follow meditation assiduously; otherwise what will happen? You will be moving about like a calf that just jumps about here and there. I insist you stabilize yourself by meditation. Your senses are very active; they are not under control. By meditating that particular weakness of your mind will be brought under control.

Q: What shall I do? For a long time I have been trying. I cannot.

M: Persistence. That deep longing must be there. If you need something very badly you think of it continuously, you are persistent about it; then you will reach that stage.

January 21, 1980

Maharaj: This consciousness is all-pervading when the touch of "I Amness" is not present. All this manifestation is for you, because you are. Since it had no support to say "I am this or that," it caught hold of the body and said "I am a male or a female."

Questioner: So the only thing you have to do is to see that you are not any of this?

M: To what extent are you going to say I am not this or that?

Q: Once one has seen it one does not have to repeat it?

M: Once you understand that you are not the body then are you not everything? Are you not the five elemental play? Whatever is you are. The message "I Am" does not have any form, design, or color. So long as "I Am," this experience of manifestation, is, once that "I Amness" disappears there is no experience. Once this message "I Am" appears, in insect, animal, or human being, immediately the manifestation occurs with that beingness. Inside and outside is full of manifestation. These talks are not for general consumption, for the masses.

Most people want to derive certain benefits from certain actions, but what happens here? For whom is anything? The whom itself gets dissolved.

I'll tell you only one thing, go on humming Guru, Guru, Guru, that is "I Amness." Go on humming "I Am" without words, the unstruck sound.

Q: How can you experience that? What is the path?

M: You recede into that. Everybody is asking for a path; how can I indicate a path? How did I enter into my mother's womb? How can I tell you? Everybody wants a path. Follow the same path by which you came.

The message "I Am" has no form; it is only a food container. It is there, it has meaning, but you cannot perceive it, observe it. I receive a letter containing all the information about myself but that message is not me. I am the observer of the message. The message "I Am" is time-bound. The principle to which "I Am" refers is beyond time, timeless, eternal.

Q: The observer is the meeting point between the time-bound and the timeless.

M: The witnessing of the manifest world happens to that Ultimate principle. When you observe something you receive it, record it, and deliberate over it; therefore you are involved in it. The Ultimate does not receive or record the passing show.

March 28, 1980

Maharaj: This knowledge "I Am" is the same, whether it is an insect, worm, human being, or an avatar [being of the highest order]; the basic consciousness is the same in all of these.

In order to manifest itself the consciousness needs a frame, a particular construct in which it can appear. That form can be anything, but it needs a form, and it lasts only as long as that particular form remains. Until that consciousness appears there cannot be any knowledge of any kind; knowledge can only be there when this base, the knowledge "I Am," is there.

Thought arises from the breath and the thought expresses itself in words. Without words there could not be any communication in the world. The world goes on because of the word and the name. People cannot be identified without a name, so the name has great importance. Even God has to be given a name, and when we repeat that name it has a certain significance. At an early stage there is no method more important or more easily successful than repeating the name of God.

Questioner: How did this consciousness come about?

M: There is no reason why this consciousness came about, but once it comes about, it cannot stand still; consciousness is the same as movement. That movement takes place through the three gunas which are inherent in this knowledge "I Am." All movement takes place through these gunas and this consciousness keeps on humming. A particular form has come about through a particular food, and through the combination of the gunas will act according to the form which it has taken. The worm will act like a worm, a man like a man, etc. The qualities are predestined. Behavior and action take place according to the combination of the three gunas.

When people first come here they come with the purpose of exhibiting their own knowledge or of drawing me into a discussion. I am aware of this and even more strongly aware that such people don't know anything; they are sheerly ignorant. For this reason I tell them not to start asking questions or discussing until they have listened to the talks for a while and absorbed at least some of what I say.

How do I know that you are completely ignorant? From my own experience. Where did all this start? It is part of the knowledge "I Am," and this knowledge and the particular form, the whole bundle, has been created out of the five elements, and the five elements have no knowledge; so the whole thing is pure ignorance.

There are some people who say, "I was so and so in a previous birth and I will come again as so and so." How do they know? All of this can only come out of the five elements, and before the five elements were created the previous knowledge could not have been—so it is all rubbish, nonsense.

There are many Hatha Yogis who have great powers; of those, I am the biggest. Hatha means persistence, insistence. What is this persistence? I didn't know I was born; how did I get this form? That is the point to be persistent about. I must know this. Then I was told Satva. What is Satva? Satva is only the essence of the five elements and in that is the knowledge "I Am." All that is still of the five elements; so how did this come about? Then my Guru told me, "This is what you are," the whole story; so from my own experience I know that it is all ignorance.

My Guru pointed out to me that originally I had nothing to do with all this and all I have with which to solve this mystery of life is the knowledge "I Am"; without that there is nothing. So I got hold of it, as my Guru told me, and then I wanted to find out how this body aspect came about without my knowledge and how on that alone can any other answer come about, and that again is the result of the five elements. Therefore, whatever anybody thinks he has is sheer ignorance, and I know it from my own experience.

If this is ignorance, then where is my beingness? My

beingness is in a town which is no-town, in a place which is no-place.

How did this come about? Because of this knowledge "I Am," which is ignorance, Maya, which came about suddenly, without my asking. Once having come about, this Maya liked what it had created and it wanted that beingness to last for all time. Maya embraced it with such fierceness, that, at any cost, it wants to prolong the existence of that beingness as long as it can.

One has an itch; what is the cause? The physical body. This itch to continue to live, to exist, comes from the five elements and will last as long as the five elemental body is present.

You think you know me and for that reason you come here, but I have no shape or form. That no-place where my true being is also has no form or shape. Whatever I speak about is only that which has come about because of the essence of the five elements, but I have nothing to do with that.

Extremely intelligent people come here and ask me questions and I answer them, but they don't accept my answers. Why? They are speaking from the point of identification with the body-mind, and I answer them without identification with the form, so how can they understand me? How can the answer tally with the question?

Who is asking the questions? That person who has measured himself from the state of time based on the birth of the physical body, which is a figment of the imagination, purely a bundle of memories, habits, and imagination. I know it, but they don't. You have been considering yourself as the body, although it has no substance and can disappear at any moment. Yet, based on it you are trying to achieve and acquire, etc. Only what was before this body came into existence will remain after the body dies. The moment the body is gone, that final day, even your memory of existence will disappear. Whatever you have assimilated is only entertainment—everything will disappear. What I said—do you agree with it?

Q: Yes.

M: If you have really accepted it, then you will not care whether the body remains or goes.

All the pride of any being is based entirely on this food essence quality, the beingness. It is a temporary phase, and in understanding this you come to the conclusion that it is unreal. The one who understands that it is unreal is the Eternal.

In this game can you hold on to some identity as exclusively yours that will not disappear?

Q: No.

Translator: These people have come here from a village and they want to take Maharaj there by car, so Maharaj asked:

M: Will anybody be able to understand this type of talk in your village?

Q: No, nobody will understand, it will go over their heads. They might be enraged at such talk and beat you.

M: No, they will not. The foreigners may try to attack me because they think that I am criticizing Christ. I am indicating to you the true position of Christ, the actual state. What was done to Christ might happen to me also, because Christ told the facts, the truth, but people became enraged and crucified him. Now they make the sign of the cross. Since my talk is beyond their understanding they will be disturbed.

At the command of my Guru I am doing these bhajans and talks. When I go to that village I shall have to talk about God and the devotee. They will not be able to understand, so I will talk at their level. For the ignorant this is all right: God is eternal, there is sin and virtue. For the ignorant all these things are true, but they are all hearsay.

It is said that God and the world are ancient, eternal. When I was not I did not know about this eternal world and God. When I was not they did not exist.

Take the example of the dream world. In the dream world I see a great spectacle of old castles, ancient monuments, but my dream is very fresh and new. I have the dream for the moment only, so how can the spectacle be ancient? Similarly, this also is for the moment. So long as the beingness is there the world is there. Without my beingness there is no world.

I believe that you are listening to my talks and understanding properly. If that be so, why should you have any fear of death? Finally, what is death? This body is like a lamp with fuel, and the wick is aflame with beingness. You know that when the fuel is exhausted the flame will disappear, the "I Amness" will disappear.

My Guru told me to be one with that beingness, and when you are one with it, that very principle will disclose to you all the mysteries of this beingness and in that process you will transcend it; but be very humble, be very devoted.

Q: This beingness, thoughts, personality, even my coming here, is a mere accident—there's no reason. Is that correct?

M: Yes. Whatever is supposedly happening is an illusion. Nothing is really happening because the basic concept, beingness, is itself an illusion.

When you escape this body-mind state you are the manifest beingness, but in that manifest state you transcend beingness also. In realizing that you are the manifest you escape beingness. You are almost in being and no-being, beyond that.

Q: Then you are nothing, the final stage?

M: Who is there to say that, who will say that he is not there and with what?

Q: The flame of beingness in the Brahma aperture—what is one to do when one feels it? Is one to ignore it or to concentrate on it?

M: Merely watch those experiences. Simply watch all that you see, be aware.

The beingness, the "I Am," is merely an instrument, it is not you. It is an instrument of knowledge, and that great instrument of knowledge is called God, which is the quality of the food essence. Out of that alone you will be able to see everything else.

Q: Did I understand that you are not to flow with the beingness and enjoy it? You pull back and watch?

M: Even if you flow with it, you are separate. You might be able to see yourself enjoying also, but still you are the watchdog, not the participant. You must remember that these experiences are due to your beingness. Beingness is only your quality and not you. You might even see that your body is lying dead there and it is a part of beingness, but you are not that. That you must realize and watch and see.

What are you now and what would you like to be?

Q: I would like to enjoy the all-pervading, to be one with it.

M: Who is it that wants to become one with that all-pervading principle? First of all, get rid of that "you." This is the place where all your hopes, expectations, and desires are completely dissolved, annihilated. At that stage what is left of you? You dabble in many concepts. So long as we are one with that beingness we would always like to have some very high concepts about ourselves.

March 29, 1980

Maharaj: Once the body comes to an end, it mixes with the five elements, the vital breath mixes with the air, and the consciousness mixes with the universal consciousness. Thereupon the consciousness which was subject to the three gunas in the body becomes free of them, becomes Nirguna. The idea of rebirth is a concept, because for something to be reborn something has to die. What is dead? Nothing is dead. Who is to be reborn? No one was born.

Whatever education you have received has been on the basis of the body-mind, so whatever concepts you have will only remain concepts. But once the body mixes with the five elements, breath mixes with the air, and consciousness becomes universal consciousness, the concepts will have no stand, no support. Therefore, where will they go?

Universal consciousness doesn't come from anywhere; it is universal. It exists in a latent form in the totality of the food. It does not come from anywhere, it is already latent, and, as soon as the form is created, automatically the life force and the consciousness are exhibited in it simultaneously.

In an infinitesimal seed the whole tree is already present in a latent state; in due course it will grow and proliferate. This seed, this chemical, this beingness, contains the whole universe of yours. Ask questions from this beingness of yours and not from what you have heard or collected.

This beingness has its own latent qualities to manifest itself into this manifestation. How does it behave in the world? Through mechanical properties; it has its own mechanical way as to how it will perform in the world. These properties are latent in the chemical principle. Take a worm, or an insect, or a rat: they make their own holes to live in. Similarly, human beings work in their own fashion. From where does it spring? It comes out of their own beingness.

Questioner: But there is only one beingness; there are not lots of individual beings.

M: Just as space is one, air is one, fire is one, similarly, consciousness is also one.

This is the outcome of the integrated combination of the five elements. Thus beingness is a product of the food essence which has come out of the five elemental flow.

At the time of conception this beingness principle—this chemical—takes a photograph of whatever the situation is. That chemical emulsion which is on the photographic film receives the impressions.

That principle has unknowingly taken the photograph. At that stage it has no intelligence; then the principle becomes mature enough and attains its very purpose, the purpose of the fetus. What is the purpose? To know itself as "I Am." That gets manifest in due course in the child.

I am telling you your true nature—you are Nirguna, like Lord Krishna. Lord Krishna was the Unborn, the Nirguna principle, just as you are.

This universal consciousness gives birth every moment to so many forms, insects, animals, human beings, all the species; and people tell us that we have had many births. Do they remember all those births? Knowingly I have no knowledge about my birth, but I am charged with being born. Actually you accept those concepts because you are afraid of death.

One who is completely rid of coming and going, and, finally, one who is completely rid of one's very own concept that "I Am", is completely liberated.

In India the sadhana is reciting the sacred name of God. Without name or title you cannot get on in the world. You are given a certain title or name for God; that name is your very own name. When you recite the name, it will proliferate and give you all the knowledge. It is your own true nature. That recitation should not be given up; whether the body lives or dies, you should continuously recite that name. Even if a stupid person recites the sacred name his eternal nature will be opened up. So when such a thing happens people will troop to him to offer their obeisance or reverence.

In India this recitation of the sacred name is very important, but in foreign countries the emphasis is placed on the intellect, with the result that foreigners are very proficient in their worldly life. This recitation of the sacred nama-mantra is a tradition of my Navanath Sampradaya. Those great Sages were not educated—they were rather naive persons; nevertheless they attained the highest.

Many people after reading *I Am That* visit my place, but when I am among the crowd they are not able to locate me, because I don't have a wonderful, splendorous personality. Finally when I go and sit on that little elevated seat, they think, "Oh, this must be the guy." But at first they look at me and through me.

Q: Since Maharaj negates the idea of previous births can samskaras be interpreted as being in this life?

M: Yes, but your friends in this birth will try to tell you that they are from previous births.

March 30, 1980

Questioner: If "I Amness" is a product of the essence of food how can Babaji's "I Amness" continue to exist without food?

Maharaj: The causal body which was born out of the food essence quality of Sri Babaji is still sustaining itself, but its cause was food only. It might be two thousand or four thousand years old; still it is sustaining itself.

In mythology also we have two personages who have perpetuated their "I Amness" for thousands of years. It is said that they are still alive somewhere; they too have the causal body that is the cell of "I Amness" formed out of food essence. Nevertheless, in spite of that long period of life, could they bring about any change in the play of the five elements? Could they arrest the flow of this creation, sustenance, and destruction? It has been going on as usual; they cannot interfere with it. They were in their causal body only, observing everything.

Q: With what does one experience the states of heaven, hell, etc., after death, when both the body and intellect dissolve?

M: How can there be experience after death since the body and intellect have dissolved? What is there to experience? If the food essence quality is completely dissolved, gone, then who proceeds further?

Q: Why is there no experience of "I Amness" from infancy until some two years, when the food body and vital breath are present? Is that early state pure consciousness?

M: It is something like an unripe mango; the sweetness is there in a dormant state but has not fully expressed itself. In the ripe mango it experiences itself. Similarly, in the child, although that "I Amness" touch is present in a dormant condition, it has not fully developed, it cannot express itself.

Q: Maharaj says that there is no rebirth of the individual—the consciousness is just expressing itself. Then he tells another that his attitude will bring many rebirths.

M: To the ignorant who are obsessed by ideas of rebirth, etc., I say, "You are going to have rebirths"; but to one who is capable of understanding I will give knowledge only.

Q: Maharaj says at one time that Brahman is not a witness and at another that Brahman is a witness.

M: What is the meaning you are desiring out of this Brahman? What do you think of this word Brahman? Brahman means the emanation of the world, simultaneously confirming that "I Am."

In this Brahman everything is illusion, but who understands that? The principle that understands, realizes, and witnesses is the Parabrahman. Witnessing happens to the Parabrahman.

In this manifest state everything is ever-changing, nothing is permanent, and all is illusion.

Now you have accepted a Guru and he has given you certain knowledge. Having accepted this knowledge, where are you proceeding to? Do you understand the import of what you have received? When did you realize your Self, your true nature? You have a bank account and you say that you have ten thousand rupees. True, the money is there but you do not have it with you. You have only the information that ten thousand rupees is credited to your account. Similarly, you have heard about your birth and death, but this information is not going to remain with you, even the information that you are is going to disappear.

You who are pursuing spirituality, go to its end, complete it; otherwise, follow your normal mode of life. You must come to the conclusion that you are the Unborn, you shall ever remain the Unborn. The world and the mind—everything—is unreal, but I am not those.

April 2, 1980

Maharaj: I was talking up and down, left and right, topsy-turvy. After listening to my talks one person was completely disappointed and frustrated, and went off. The next day he came back again, challenging me. So I told him, "Oh yes, your talk is very profound. If only you had met me a little earlier, I would have made you my Guru." Then he was very happy.

Questioner: Maharaj said that without food there is no beingness, but I thought beingness and consciousness were always present. That is the Absolute; so it's not the same as food or material things.

M: Everything is this consciousness, but one is not aware of the consciousness unless there is a body. The knowledge of being does not come about unless there is a form, and that form cannot maintain itself unless there is food.

Q: Does consciousness depend on form?

M: Consciousness is present everywhere, but knowledge of that consciousness is dependent on the form.

Q: Pure consciousness, without form, is impossible then?

M: Consciousness is present, but not the knowledge of it. Who will have the knowledge?

Q: But yesterday Maharaj said to stick to the knowledge "I Am"; that would be sticking to the material form.

M: There is no question of hanging on to it, it is there—you can't get away from it.

Q: What should I meditate on then?

M: Remain quiet in the consciousness. The one who understands the quality of this beingness transcends it and is no more affected by birth or death.

Q: Without consciousness what remains?

M: The Absolute state, out of which the five elements take shape or form; when the movement is frozen but the potential is present. That is Parabrahman; there is no movement.

Q: But there is nothing conscious about it?

M: The Absolute does not know Itself. Without the aid of the food essence, body consciousness does not know itself. Nobody knows himself without the food essence body.

Q: Maharaj is in the Absolute state, so is he not aware of himself?

M: I know that state forever.

Q: But you said It did not know Itself.

M: If that state alone prevails It will not know Itself, but when this body and beingness is available It is known through them.

Q: But when the body disappears?

M: No-knowing.

Q: Then when Maharaj is dead he doesn't know the Absolute state anymore?

M: All this play is in the realm of the five elements. Death means what? This body and beingness will merge in the five elements.

The Absolute has the aid of this five elemental beingness and body available to It to express Itself, but beingness is made up of the raw material of the five elements. The Absolute has nothing to do with it except to express Itself through that.

In mundane, worldly matters you have recourse to spirituality to understand how unreal this is. Once you understand the object of spirituality, you also understand that spirituality is unreal, and in the process you dismiss all this world.

I am telling you in plain and simple language: Here is the food that is served; in that food this "I Amness" is in a dormant condition. It only peeks out when it has a body. Unfortunately, you are trying to identify with this food product; therefore all the trouble starts.

Q: If Maharaj goes for a walk and stumbles over both a rock and a crippled beggar boy, are they the same to him?

M: About what would I make a difference? Who are you calling a rock and who a boy? I am not an individual. What is your question?

Q: Then Maharaj would not be concerned?

M: The point which you must understand is that there is no individual personality. Out of the essence of the five elements all form and beingness come. Forget about Maharaj; there is no difference.

The body, or beingness, is going to respond in the natural way for that beingness. I, the Absolute, am not concerned with its response. When the child is a few days old it is the quintessence of the food essence only. After a few months, it develops the sense of knowledge and receives impressions. Those impressions are registered, like a photograph, in that chemical. Then the five senses of action also do their part and receive more impressions. Later on the reactions take place accordingly.

Q: Is it a law? Must it happen this way?

M: All this play is mechanical, a part of the chemical. Birth means the formation of that chemical. The quintessence of the food body is the chemical, which is necessary for the consciousness to appear, to feel "I Am." Do you understand now?

Q: I understand now. But I think Maharaj must be joking. He says he sees no difference between the stone and the beggar boy, yet he spends hours and hours teaching stupid people; and there are bhajans, day after day after day, with no vacation, but he says "It happens." I think he must be joking.

M: This is all a joke.

Translator: That "I Am" quality in Maharaj is suffering at seeing the ignorance of others. That quality of his beingness likes to help others. It does not like to see the suffering born out of ignorance.

Q: Why not?

M: Because the beingness will act according to its own nature. That is its nature.

Q: That's rather queer. Most people, or their chemicals, simply want to serve themselves, but his chemicals are so special that they want to help others.

M: That by which you know you are is due to what?

Q: Body consciousness, the chemicals, etc.

M: You are not focusing your attention on that beingness principle. Just be there. In that beingness everything is happening, but you, the Absolute, are not that. You will understand gradually.

Q: I know I am not my finger, but I would not bite it off.

M: Don't take any action. UNDERSTAND. You are again trying to act as an individual. To understand what I am telling you it is imperative that you have recourse to meditation.

Don't be carried away by concepts, just dwell in the quietude.

Glossary

Advaita: Non-duality.

Adya: Primordial; original.

Agni: Fire.

Aham: I; the ego.

Ajnana: Ignorance.

Akasha: Ether.

Ananda: Bliss; happiness; joy.

Arati: Divine service performed in the early morning or at dusk.

Asana: Posture; seat.

Ashram: Hermitage.

Atma: The Self.

Avatar: Divine incarnation.

Bhagavan: The Lord.

Bhajan: Worship [of the Lord].

Bhakta: Devotee; votary.

Bhakti: Devotion; love [of God].

Bija: Seed; source.

Brahman: God as creator.

Brahma-randhra: Opening in the crown of the head; fontanelle.

Buddhi: Intellect.

Chaitanya: Consciousness.

Chakra: Plexus.

Chit: Universal consciousness.

Chitakasa: Mental ether [all-pervading].

Chitta: Mind stuff.

Deva: Divine being.

Dhyana: Meditation; contemplation.

Ganapati: A Hindu deity; success-bestowing aspect of God.

Gayatri: Sacred Vedic mantra.

Gita: Song.

Guna: Quality born of nature.

Guru: Teacher; preceptor.

Hanuman: A powerful deity; the son of the Wind God; a great devotee of Sri Rama; the famous monkey who helped Rama in his fight with Ravana.

Hatha Yoga: A system of Yoga for gaining control over the physical body and Prana.

Hetu: Cause; reason.

Hiranyagarbha: Cosmic intelligence; cosmic mind; cosmic egg.

Iswara: God.

Jagat: World; changing.

Jagrat: Waking condition.

Japa: Repetition of God's name; repetition of a mantra.

Jiva: Individual soul.

Jnana: Knowledge.

Kalpana: Imagination of the mind; creation.

Kama: Desire; lust.

Karma: Action.

Karta: Doer.

Kendra: Center; heart.

Kosa: Sheath.

Kriya: Physical action.

Kumbhaka: Retention of breath.

Kundalini: The primordial cosmic energy located in the individual.

Laya: Dissolution; merging.

Lila: Play; sport.

Linga: Symbol.

Maha: Great.

Mahattava: The great principle.

Mahesvara: Great Lord.

Manana: Constant thinking; reflection; meditation.

Manas: Mind, the thinking faculty.

Manolaya: Involution and dissolution of the mind into its cause.

Mantra: Sacred syllable or word or set of words.

Marga: Path or road.

Mauna or *Mouna:* Silence.

Maya: The illusive power of Brahman; the veiling and pro-
     jecting power of the universe.

Moksha or *Mukti:* Release; liberation.

Mouna: See *Mauna.*

Mukti: See *Moksha.*

Mula: Origin; root; base.

Mumukshu: Seeker after liberation.

Muni: A sage; an austere person.

Murti: Idol.

Nada: Mystic sound.

Nadi: Nerve; psychic current.

Nama: Name.

Namarupa: Name and form; the nature of the world.

Neti-neti: "Not this, not this"; negating all names and forms
     in order to arrive at the eternal underlying truth.

Nirguna: Without attributes.

Nirgunabrahman: The impersonal, attributeless Absolute.

Nirvana: Liberation; final emancipation.

Nirvikappa: Without the modifications of the mind.

Niskama: Without desire.

Pandit: A learned man; a scholar; a man of wisdom.

Para: Supreme; other.

Parabrahman: The Supreme Absolute.

Prajna: Consciousness; awareness.

Prakriti: Causal matter; also called shakti.

Pralaya: Complete merging; dissolution.

Prana: Vital energy; life breath.

Prema: Divine love [for God].

Puja: Worship.

Purna: Full; complete; infinite.

Purusa: The Self which abides in the heart of all things.

Rajas: One of the three aspects of cosmic energy; passion;
     restlessness.

Sadhaka: Spiritual aspirant.

Sadhana: Spiritual practice.

Sadhu: Pious or righteous man; a Sanyasin.

Sagunabrahman: The Absolute conceived of as endowed with qualities.

Sakti or *Shakti:* Power; energy; force.

Samadhi: Oneness; here the mind becomes identified with the object of meditation.

Samsara: The process of worldly life.

Samskara: Impression.

Sankalpa: Thought; desire; imagination.

Sastra: See *Shastra*.

Sat: Existence; being; reality.

Sat-chit-ananda: Existence-knowledge-bliss.

Satsang: Association with the wise.

Satva or *Sattwa:* Light; purity.

Shakti: See *Prakriti; Sakti*.

Shastra or *Sastra:* Scripture.

Siddha: A perfected Yogi.

Siddhi: Psychic power.

Sloka: Verse of praise.

Sphurna: Throbbing or breaking; bursting forth; vibration.

Sunya: Void.

Susumna: The important nerve current that passes through the spinal column through which the kundalini rises.

Susupti: Deep sleep.

Sutra: A terse sentence.

Swarupa: Essence; essential nature; true nature of Being.

Tattva: Element; essence; principle.

Turiya: Superconscious state.

Upanishad: Knowledge portion of the Vedas.

Vac or *Vak:* Speech.

Vaikuntha: The abode of Lord Vishnu.

Vairagya: Indifference toward all worldly things.

Vak: See *Vac*.

Vasana: Subtle desire.

Vayu: The Wind God; air; vital breath.

Veda: A scripture of the Hindus.

Vedanta: The end of the Vedas.

Vichara: Inquiry into the nature of the Self.

Vidya: Knowledge [of Brahman].

Vijnana: Principle of pure intelligence.

Virat: Macrocosm; the physical world.

Viveka: Discrimination between the Real and the unreal.

Vritti: Thought-wave; mental modification.

Vyasa: The name of a great sage who wrote the Brahma Sutras.

Yama: God of Death.

Yoga: Union; the philosophy of the sage Paranjali teaching the union of the individual with God.

Yogi: One who practices Yoga.